EUROPEAN SOCIAL CLASS:
STABILITY AND CHANGE

MAIN THEMES IN EUROPEAN HISTORY

Bruce Mazlish, General Editor

Other volumes in preparation

EUROPEAN SOCIAL CLASS:
STABILITY AND CHANGE

BERNARD BARBER
Barnard College, Columbia University

and

ELINOR G. BARBER
International Encyclopedia of the Social Sciences

THE MACMILLAN COMPANY, NEW YORK

To Crane Brinton

FOREWORD

History, we are frequently told, is a seamless web. However, by isolating and studying the strands that compose the tapestry of man's past, we are able to discern the pattern, or patterns, of which it is comprised. Such an effort does not preclude a grasp of the warp and woof, and the interplay of the strands; rather, it eventually demands and facilitates such a comprehension. It is with this in mind that the individual volumes of the MAIN THEMES series have been conceived.

The student will discover, for example, that the population changes discussed in one volume relate to the changes in technology traced in another volume; that both changes are affected by, and affect in turn, religious and intellectual developments; and that all of these changes and many more ramify into a complicated historical network through all the volumes. In following through this complex interrelationship of parts, the student recreates for himself the unity of history.

Each volume achieves its purpose, and its appeal to a general audience, by presenting the best articles by experts in the field of history and allied disciplines. In a number of cases, the articles have been translated into English for the first time. The individual volume editor has linked these contributions into an integrated account of his theme, and supplied a selected bibliography by means of footnotes for the student who wishes to pursue the topic further. The introduction is an original treatment of the problems in the particular field. It provides continuity and background for the articles, points out gaps in the existing literature, offers new interpretations, and suggests further research.

The volumes in this series afford the student of history an unusual opportunity to explore subjects either not treated, or touched upon lightly in a survey text. Some examples are population—the dramatis personae of history; war—the way of waging peace by other means;

the rise of technology and science in relation to society; the role of religious and cultural ideas and institutions; the continuous ebb and flow of exploration and colonialism; and the political and economic works contrived by modern man. Holding fast to these Ariadne threads, the student penetrates the fascinating labyrinth of history.

BRUCE MAZLISH
General Editor

TABLE OF CONTENTS

EUROPEAN SOCIAL CLASS: STABILITY AND CHANGE

INTRODUCTION

For a long time now the language of social class has been one of the important modes of description and explanation in European historiography. Indeed, as Hexter points out in his essay "The Myth of the Rising Middle Class," this language has been used by Marxists and non-Marxists alike.* A good deal of this usage, chiefly the Marxist, has been informed with an explicit ideological intent. The rest, though intended to be more objective, unfortunately has often been at no more than a commonsense level of interpretation. All too frequently, both kinds of intention have not been combined with good historical research but have rested instead on the repetition of historical clichés.

The essays included in this collection of writings about European social stratification represent an improvement in historical scholarship in each of two different respects. First, nearly all of them exemplify historical research at its best: detailed, exhaustive, accurate, up-to-date. Second, they use newer and better ideas or concepts, and in some cases newer quantitative research techniques, to deal with historical materials that formerly were inadequately treated by ideological or commonsense preconceptions.

These essays also attempt a further improvement over older work. They deal in a more satisfactory way with the processes of stability and change in European stratification systems over the last six centuries. Formerly, the transformations of these systems during this period were treated as if they had been sudden, single, and simple. In these newer analyses, we have moved toward an historical picture that reveals the slowness of these transformations, their complexity, and the diversity and frequent incongruity of their subprocesses.

What are the several different aspects of stratification systems we ought to keep in mind when we study European societies historically? What elements of stability and change in each of these can we discern in the materials that historical research has already disclosed to us? And, finally, what new kinds of historical research are necessary on different aspects of stratification systems and on different European countries? These are some questions we shall try to answer briefly in

---

* No material from Marxist writings has been included here because of its ready availability elsewhere and its general familiarity.

this introductory essay, pointing wherever possible to the essays that follow. Lest there be misunderstanding on this score, we must emphasize that the order in which we discuss the several different aspects of stratification systems is not in order of their relative importance. As different aspects of an institutional system, they are in principle equally important, though in historical fact they can vary in different historical circumstances. Our order is one of didactic convenience.

Differential Evaluation of Occupational Roles

In all societies there is differential evaluation of the occupational roles that men have to fill as a normal and necessary part of their daily lives. Generals are more highly esteemed than corporals; and governmental officials, rank for equal rank, may be esteemed more than businessmen. Differential evaluation occurs even when important functional activities which nowadays we should call "occupations," such as landowning-and-managing or being a priest, were not thought of as "occupations" in earlier historical periods. During the last six centuries of European history there has been a basic change in the structure of differential evaluation of occupational roles. In the earlier part of this period, the military, landowning-and-managing, governmental, and religious official roles were more highly evaluated than commercial, industrial, scientific, teaching, and various other professional roles. This is not to say that these latter roles carried no value at all; far from it, as the essays by Stone, Ohlin, Hexter, and Reinhard make clear. But because they used to be relatively less valued in European societies, these were roles that men sought to escape if they could. As soon as men accumulated enough wealth in business or professional roles, they moved "upward," as they themselves and those whom they admired defined it, into the landowning-and-managing, the military, and the governmental roles. In some countries, indeed, though not in all, and with important consequences for these different countries, the landowning nobility did not disdain to engage in commerce or industry or mining so long as it was recognized as a secondary activity, a way of giving some support to their primary and "more noble" activities. In England and Sweden, as both Stone and Ohlin point out, or in Italy, bourgeois activities carried less of a stigma than in France or Spain, where, until the end of the seventeenth century, noble status was jeopardized by commercial activity. It would be good to have further research on the subtle but important differences in relative evaluation of this kind in the different European countries and to trace out the effects such differences had on the relative rates of modernization of these countries.

Gradually, and everywhere, the functional importance, the number and the relative prestige of "modern" occupational roles increased in all countries, but the gradual processes involved have not been precisely charted in the way in which, say, the gradual processes of governmental transformation have been studied. Such a charting would make very clear that the preference for the "older" roles, such as landowning-and-managing and military roles, did not suddenly and totally disappear. Some of this preference, even a good deal, as we are told by Aydelotte and Landes, persisted far into the nineteenth century in England and especially France.

The Structure or Shape of the Stratification System

The differential evaluations of occupational roles that are one aspect of a stratification system bring about a second aspect, its structure or shape. If these differential evaluations define as high-ranking only a few types of roles, with few occupants; if they define as middle-ranking a somewhat larger but still small number of types of roles; and if they define as low-ranking all other types of roles, containing the vast majority of members of the society, then we say that the structure or shape of the stratification system is pyramidal. This is the shape that has characterized all European stratification systems until quite recently. Stone's description of the class structure of sixteenth and seventeenth century England provides a good illustration.

But gradually the shape of European stratification systems has changed, though again we do not have any precise charting of the gradual processes that altered structures without suddenly and all at once undermining the stability of the systems. As the importance and number of the more "modern" business and professional roles has increased, not only has there been a change in the *type* of role that is most highly esteemed, but there has been a proportionately greater *number* of middle-ranking roles. The stratification systems of Europe have moved from a pyramidal to a diamond shape, one in which the proportions of people filling middle-ranking roles are far larger than those in either the highest-ranking or lowest-ranking roles. This is what is often meant when we refer to modern European societies as "middle class," namely, that the greatest proportion of people are in these new ranks and roles. So large is the proportion of people in these roles that some writers have even spoken of "the middle mass." In any modern society, the great majority of people will be "white collar" and middle-ranking. This does not mean that all distinctions have ceased or that it is appropriate to treat all "white collar" or "middle class" people as equal. As always, subtle but important differences of evaluation are made, both of oneself and of one's fellows, depending upon the different functional significance of various occupations. Middle-level corporation executives are ranked higher than white-collar foremen who work for them. It may be, of course, that the proliferation of middle-ranking roles sometimes makes it hard to make different evaluations of two or more occupations, especially when these are esoteric and therefore rankable only by experts. Where this occurs, actual inequalities are less publicly visible; such obscurities of social-class ranking contribute to the feeling of equality nearly all of us value for its own sake.

Like any hierarchy, whether pyramidal or diamond-like, the structure of European and other modern stratification systems has a definite tendency to taper off sharply at the peak. Reinhard's essay shows that although the French Revolution modified the composition of the elite, the elite remained of necessity a small group. This tendency to peaking occurs in all modern societies—socialist, communist, capitalist, and mixed—and its necessity clashes with the value of equality. However, men have generally worked out tolerable accommodations to the dilemma that complete equality and functionally necessary differentiation are incompatible with one another.

Amounts of Mobility

A third aspect of any stratification system is the amount of mobility that occurs within it. Mobility is defined as the movement by a man into an occupational position that is either more or less valued than the one his father held. Some mobility, we now recognize, occurs in all types of stratification systems, even the Hindu caste system. Recent historical research on European stratification systems has also changed our view of how much mobility occurred in early modern times; we now know that the amount was intermediate between the minimum amount that occurs in the caste type of system and the maximum amount that occurs in contemporary open-class systems. This intermediate amount of mobility was both consequence and cause of the many different types of social process and change that were present in early modern times.

In general, we can see that the European societies of that time were more dynamic than we used to think.

But this intermediate amount of mobility was not necessarily the cause of basic transformation in other aspects of European stratification systems. That is to say, for a long time, as Hexter so forcefully argues, a steady flow of social mobility into and out of the bourgeoisie or middle class occurred without a transformation either of the relative evaluation of different types of social roles or of the shape of the stratification system as a whole. Eventually, of course, these different aspects of the stratification system did affect one another, but not until the later eighteenth and the nineteenth centuries. On the one hand, the higher evaluation of "modern" roles gradually created more opportunities for social mobility; so also did the greater opportunity-structure that was represented by the diamond-like rather than the pyramidal shape of the stratification system. On the othet hand, as more men tried to rise, they created more opportunities and redefined the worth of the new roles they sought to enter. So far we have little good historical evidence on just when these reciprocal effects began to occur, and at what rate. We do know that certain amounts of social mobility can occur without transforming the stratification system as a whole. Failure to perceive this possibility was what misled many historians into seeing every instance of *individual* social mobility from the bourgeoisie into the nobility from the Middle Ages onward as a proof of *the rising of the middle classes*.

For the measurement of the amount of social mobility, it is necessary to ascertain the amount of downward mobility as well as of upward. Sometimes the two amounts will balance, when the stratification system is relatively stable. But whenever the opportunity-structure that the stratification system represents is either contracting or expanding, the two amounts will differ in size. In recent times, as European opportunity-structures have expanded, the amount of upward mobility has generally exceeded the downward, though there have been short-run countertrends, as during great depressions.

Degrees of Mobility

Some instances of mobility represent movement from one occupational position to another that is ranked only a little higher or lower; other instances represent movement between positions that are much farther apart. This is what we mean by degrees of mobility, the relative distance between two differently ranked positions that mobility covers. Although we have sometimes concentrated on the mobility of large degree in very recent times—what has been called in American society, Horatio Alger mobility—we now know from a good deal of historical research that such mobility does not occur very often, even in American society. The best estimate is that something like 3 to 4 percent of all mobility is of large degree. The remaining mobility is of small degree, representing movement between adjacent or nearly adjacent occupational positions. In the early modern period of European history, probably an even greater proportion of the mobility that occured was mobility of very small degree, though we do not have good measures of the amounts of mobility of different degree for any places or any times outside of recent America. As Hecht shows in his study of social mobility among the servants of eighteenth century England, people moved up only a little in each generation. The rise of the father might provide a slightly higher base for the further rise of the son, and so on through several succeeding generations. Nevertheless, even in earlier times there were cases of movement of larger degree, instance the servant Robert Dodsley whose history Hecht gives. Especially in times of war and social disturbance, when talent was more urgently in demand and when the stable social structure had been knocked awry, some men could move up very far, or down the same distance, in the stratification system. But even in the French Revolution, it was nearly always the already middle-ranking lawyer who moved up into the top-ranking positions from which the nobility had been driven, not the proletarian or even the artisan.

Processes or Channels of Mobility

In the early part of the period of European history that our essays cover, mobility was restricted to a few typical channels, which are, on the whole, different from the typical channels of contemporary Europe. Men could move up through military or governmental service, as Rosenberg shows in great detail in the case of Prussia. Some men could still rise in the Church, though most of the higher positions were reserved for the sons of the nobility. And finally, as both Stone and Hexter show, men could move up by using the profits of their success in commerce and industry to buy landed estates for themselves and to purchase military commissions and other offices for their sons.

Gradually, however, as "modern" roles became more important in the stratification systems of Europe, individual achievement came to be still more significant for mobility than it had been in earlier times. Rising through the military, the government, or the churches was still possible, but there were now many more opportunities in business and the professions. Also, across the stratification system, education became an increasingly essential prerequisite, both for social mobility and for maintaining the high position into which one was born. As the study by Jenkins and Jones shows, the English landowning nobility and gentry went to the universities in increasing numbers, sometimes to learn what they needed to know about new techniques of agricultural management, sometimes to learn what was necessary for entrance into the civil service or the free professions. In increasing numbers also, the sons of the middle class—business, professional, and governmental alike—went to the university in hope of further advancing the processes of social mobility which their fathers had begun.

Both Aydelotte's data and the findings of Jenkins and Jones show how individual families could maintain a certain stability in their social class position despite changes in the relative evaluation of certain types of occupational roles or changes in the opportunity-structures for those roles. Both studies give us quantitative evidence on how the nobility and gentry of England used their established high positions and wealth to get for their sons the education they needed for the new types of occupations and to get for themselves the businesses that were becoming the only possible alternative to landowning-and-managing as a way of maintaining a high social class position. Similarly, Reinhard's account of French society before, during, and just after the Revolution shows that upper-class families can sometimes maintain their relative standing throughout periods of extreme social turmoil.

Norms About Mobility

The amounts and degrees of mobility in a society are the products not only of the opportunity-structure provided by the existing occupational roles but also of the norms about social mobility, the norms that either approve or disapprove of mobility. Even though we know something about these norms at different times and places as they were expressed in the writings of the well-educated upper classes, we know little, directly, about how other people in the society felt, although it seems to be a safe guess that the lower classes had pretty much the same norms as the upper classes. For the present, of course, public opinion polls that sample a representative cross section of a national population tell us what the several different classes of the society feel about social mobility.

Until quite recently, the predominant type of norm concerning attitudes toward social mobility has been what has been called the "caste" norm—that is, a norm that disapproves of social mobility. Only very recently has the "open-class" type of norm, which approves of mobility, been predominant in European societies, and we should remember that it is not universal even now. The very strong value we place upon equality—equality of opportunity and, in lesser degree, of condition—is a very recent development in European history. In earlier times, and certainly before the French Revolution, inequalitarian norms were supported by an organic ideology of society, an ideology that justified not only the fixity of the system itself but the appropriateness of the particular place occupied by each individual and class in the system. Such mobility as occurred was more often the result of a favorable opportunity-structure and of individual striving than of normative approval, even by the upwardly mobile individual himself. Elinor Barber shows the self-conscious ambivalence of the eighteenth century bourgeois adopting a noble style of life; his self-consciousness was justified: the "parvenu," the "bourgeois gentilhomme," were figures of scorn and fun because they had violated the norms that disapproved of mobility. In contrast, the "self-made man" is a modern hero, though not everywhere in the same measure.

Income Distribution and Minimum Welfare Standards

The shape of the income distribution is another aspect of stratification systems that varies to some extent independently. This independence always causes incongruities between the relative level of income and the relative level of prestige of some individuals. Societies usually provide some mechanisms for adjusting these incongruities. For example, even during the nineteenth century, wealthy bourgeois could use their money to buy titles, roles, and marriage partners that gave them prestige more nearly congruent with their wealth.

Like the structure of differential evaluations, the shape of income distribution tends to taper off to a peak, so that there are always some people in a society who have a great deal more money income or other rewards than the great majority. However, in its middle and lower reaches, the income distribution structure may contain varying proportions of the population. Undoubtedly there has been a trend in European societies to an increase in the proportion of people of middling income and a decrease in the proportion of those of lowest income, though in absolute terms the number of people in the lowest income categories is still considerable.

One other important trend, deriving both from our egalitarian values and from our actual increase in wealth, has been the constant rise in what we define as the minimum welfare standard for European societies, that is to say, what we feel is the lowest level of goods and services which the poorest or most helpless family in the society should have. Government welfare and social security agencies—national, regional, and local—jointly provide benefits to helpless and temporarily unemployed citizens that maintain them at least at the minimum welfare standard. This is one part of what we mean by the phrase "the welfare state." However, we should remember that despite the continual rise in the minimum welfare standard, over the last century especially, the people who are at or near that minimum standard remain very poor in terms of the goods and services available to their contemporaries who are better rewarded. Poverty remains a problem in European societies.

Style of Life

In all societies the different social classes are characterized by different styles of life, by the different kinds of things they do and by the different possessions they have. Almost anything can become an indicator of a class-typed style of life, but visible consumption items are likely to be the ones that are frequently remarked on. That is why, when he was talking about social class differences in styles of life, Veblen spoke of "conspicuous consumption." In the general sense, all classes consume conspicuously.

Because of the pyramidal distribution of income and the greater scarcity of consumer goods in the early modern period of European history, the differences in styles of life of the different classes were more marked than they are today. Also, because men were anxious to keep the classes more distinct from one another than we care to, they tried to control access to important items of the different styles of life by informal custom and sumptuary legislation. Thus, the wearing of fur was sometimes legally restricted to the nobility. But the richest and nobility-aspiring bourgeois wore it anyway. In Elinor Barber's account of the bourgeois and noble styles of life in eighteenth century France, we have a vivid account of the differences between the two, and of how they indicated important differences in class occupations, values, and attitudes. In that account we see also that the bourgeois who wanted to rise in the world, to become ennobled, often adopted the noble style of life even before he acquired his patent of noble status.

In the most recent historical period, class differences in styles of life have not disappeared but have become somewhat more subtle than they used to be. This is what people are trying to indicate when they say that nowadays we have "inconspicuous consumption." Consumption is never totally inconspicuous, never completely without significance as an indicator of relative class position, but there are degrees of conspicuousness. In Veblen's time, some of the newly risen captains of industry tried to make their class position as conspicuous as possible through elaborate consumption of all kinds. Nowadays, a great many people try to reduce the conspicuousness of their consumption as an indicator of social class position. Why should this be so? Partly it is because more people hold the value of equality and want to play down the visibility of the differences that exist and that contradict equality. Partly it is because people now use consumption as a demonstration of social characteristics other than class, for example, their education, or their cultural talents, or their recreational interests. As far as the actual class structure of modern European societies is concerned, the trend has been and continues toward what might be called *the pattern of gross equality and subtle inequality*. With regard to class differences in styles of life, the same trend seems to be in process. Sometimes it looks as if all the different classes, or at least a large portion of the middle classes, consume in exactly the same way, follow the same style of life, but when we look closer we see all the subtle differences or inequalities that are accurate indicators of the actual differences in class position.

The Structure of Power

One final aspect of any stratification system is the structure of power. Despite a very great deal of discussion in historical writing of the structure of power, we do not, unfortunately, have many objective or precise accounts of what the structure of power was in different times or places. Such accounts remain one of the essential tasks for new historical research. Rough pictures, of course, we do have, and for some purposes they are enough, but we can do much better.

We know, of course, as both Stone and Hexter point out, that there was no question of the predominant place of the nobility in the power structure of European societies in early modern times. Power struggles tended to be among segments of the nobility, or between the monarchy and the nobility, not between the nobility and the bourgeoisie, as some would have it. We know also that gradually in most places—more suddenly in France—predominant power moved from the landowning nobility to those who occupied the more "modern" roles, the industrialists and businessmen, the civil servants, and the professionals of all kinds. And we know, finally, that as the enfranchisement of the majority of the population took place in all European countries, usually not before our own century, power became still more widely shared, with the working classes and the lower white collar groups increasing their relative influence. Where most men could vote, and where there was a genuinely democratic government, the masses could pool their individually small bits of power and wield a total power great enough to have at least a countervailing and sometimes a predominant power over those in the higher social classes. Some men, such as Ortega y Gasset, who do not like this development, have complained about this "revolt of the masses," this movement of the majority into not only political but cultural power. But it seems futile to complain against a transformation of the power structure that follows inevitably from changes in other aspects of the social stratification system and that speeds those other changes along. In all its different aspects the new type of stratification system is an essential part of our new kind of society.

In conclusion, it may be desirable to stress a theme already several times touched upon. That theme is that the requisites for a satisfactory account of the transformations of European social stratification from 1500 to the present do not yet exist. Not all the different aspects of social stratification systems have been recognized for what they are—as important and somewhat independent of one another as well as being parts of a system. Nor have historical materials been collected by European historians even for those elements of stratification systems that have been recognized as important. Nevertheless, the selections that follow reveal how rewardingly some pioneers have worked on these problems. These selections are not only valuable in themselves, as accounts of the historical process, but they lay out paths for other historians to follow.

CLASS DIVISIONS IN ENGLAND, 1540–1640 *

Lawrence Stone

In the broader, more ideologically tinged, contemporary view of the stratification system of England in the sixteenth and seventeenth centuries, there were only two classes, the gentlemen or well-born, and all others. In a narrower, more historically accurate, and less ideological view, we can see that there were many subdivisions within each of these two broader classes; indeed, they overlapped. Apparently there was a basic acceptance by all men of the existing class structure. So far as men had any wish for change, it was only to change their own position upward, to rise within the established structure, not to destroy that structure in any essentials. There was, to match these aspirations, a continual though small flow of upward mobility, as well as a similar downward flow.

This class structure and these mobility processes were not basically dissimilar from what existed elsewhere in Europe at this time. Further historical research will and should bring out the subtle and, for some purposes, important differences between other countries and England. But the similarity seems to be fundamental and should be the context in which all else is seen.

Stone's account of the class structure of sixteenth and seventeenth century England focusses on the peerage; he combines outstanding historical research and the most recent sociological theory of stratification in a way that is still not common enough in the writing of history.

Lawrence Stone is an Englishman who, after some years as a Fellow of Wadham College, Oxford, has become Professor of History at Princeton University. He specializes in the social and economic history of Tudor and Stuart England.

---

* From Lawrence Stone, *The Crisis of the Aristocracy, 1540–1640,* Oxford: The Clarendon Press, 1964. Reprinted by permission.

Taking the broad view, this was a two-class society of those who were gentlemen and those who were not. As a contemporary put it with disarming simplicity 'All sortes of people created from the beginninge are devided into 2: Noble and Ignoble.' Objectors to this theory, who pointed out that all were descendants of Adam, were brushed off with the argument that 'As Adam had sonnes of honnour, soe had hee Caine destinated to dishonour'. By the end of the sixteenth century this naïve view did not even begin to fit the facts. From Sir Thomas Smith in 1583 to Sir John Doderidge in 1652, acute observers of the contemporary scene took a less idealized view of the situation.

In these days he is a Gentleman who is commonly taken and reputed. And whosoever studieth in the Universities, who professeth the liberall sciences and to be short who can live idly and without manuall labour and will beare the Port charge and countenance of a Gentleman, he shall be called Master. . . . And if need be, a King of Heralds shall give him for money armes newly made and invested with the Creast and all: the title whereof shall pretend to have bin found by the said Herauld in the perusing and viewing of old Registers.[1]

By 1640 the situation is complicated by the large number of persons who were describing themselves as 'gent.' or 'master' without reference to the Heralds, and without any pretension to a coat of arms. Small merchants, shopkeepers in provincial towns, and minor officials in government office were so styled, although they were still below the line in public repute, and would hardly have considered themselves in a position to converse on equal terms with, marry their children to, or to challenge to a duel, a true landed gentleman or esquire.

Despite the blurring of the line by the devaluation of the word 'gent.', despite the relative ease with which it could be crossed, the division between the gentleman and the rest was basic to Elizabethan society. An essential prerequisite for membership of the élite was financial independence, the capacity to live idly without the necessity of undertaking manual, mechanic, or even professional tasks. But other equally important qualifications were birth, education, and willingness to adopt the way of life and the system of values which prevailed among the landed classes. Moreover, the source of wealth was just as important as the amount, as many a great London merchant was mortified to discover. When Francis Bacon spoke contemptuously of 'such worms of Alderman' and expressed his surprise at Lionel Cranfield's tact and

[1] Sir John Doderidge, *Honors Pedigree*, 1652, pp. 147–8.

ability, 'more indeed than I could have looked for from a man of his breeding', he was merely giving voice to conventional wisdom. 'All the people which be in our contrie be either gentlemen or of the commonalty. The common is devided into marchauntes and manuaries generally, what partition soever is the sibdivident', wrote the great headmaster Richard Mulcaster, in 1581.[2]

This fundamental social division was therefore not based exclusively on wealth—indeed social divisions never are—even though achievement or retention of the higher status was impossible without it. Money was the means of acquiring and retaining status, but it was not the essence of it: the acid test was the mode of life, a concept that involved many factors. Living on a private income was one, but more important was spending liberally, dressing elegantly, and entertaining lavishly. Another was having sufficient education to display a reasonable knowledge of public affairs, and to be able to perform gracefully on the dance floor and on horseback, in the tennis-court and the fencing school. By the early seventeenth century it even included table manners, as is shown by the story of how the Earl of Carlisle dropped a man because he took a knife out of his pocket to cut his meat, 'the cognisance of a clowne'.

Above and below this fundamental cleavage there were a series of important subdivisions which split both the minority at the top and the majority at the bottom. Elizabethan and Early Stuart society can best be regarded either as a two-tiered system, as hitherto we have treated it, or as a seven-tiered system, each individual being ranked within his group according to the antiquity of his arrival into it, his personal talents, and his wealth. At the very bottom there was the vagrant, the cottager, the hired labourer, the household servant, and the industrial and commercial wage-earner in factory, mine, or shop— a group which probably comprised well over half the population. One degree above was the small freeholder or leaseholder, the self-employed artisan, the shopkeeper and the internal trader. These two together formed the lower groups below the level of the gentry. Next there was an indeterminate, transitional, group consisting of the hundred-odd great export merchants of London, Exeter, Bristol, and a very few other major ports. These great merchants were far from dominating the social, much less the political, scene. Despite their wealth, they lacked confidence in their status and pride in their occupation; their chief ambition was to pull out of trade, buy an estate, and become absorbed into the landed gentry. As a result they are the most fluid and transi-

[2] R. Mulcaster, *Positions*, 1581, p. 198.

tory of classes, if indeed they can be called a class at all. The majority younger sons of yeomen or lesser gentry, they spent their working lives in a quite different environment and occupation; and in late middle age most of them deliberately cut loose and bought their way back into the country-side at a higher social level.

The upper classes, which comprised the top 5 per cent. or so of the population, divided into three broad groups roughly defined by rank. The first were the plain gentlemen, mostly small, landed proprietors but also in part professional men, civil servants, lawyers, higher clergy, and university dons. Above them were the county *élite*—many of the esquires and nearly all the knights and baronets, titular categories which expanded enormously in numbers, in the early seventeenth century, and which in purely economic terms have an awkward tendency to merge into one another. Finally at the top there were the 60 to 120 members of the titular peerage, itself subdivided into a higher and lower subsection. In this three-tiered division of the gentle classes, the upper gentry are important as forming the link between the other two. They are the men who controlled county politics under the patronage of the local nobleman, who provided the M.P.s and Deputy Lieutenants, and who dominated the bench of Justices. In a large southern county they seem to have comprised about 20 to 25 families, the total being therefore some 500 in all in the whole country. This group has been clearly identified in recent studies of Somerset, Wiltshire, Norfolk, and Kent, being distinguished by wealth, political influence, and style of living.[3] These 500 upper gentry families are in many ways similar in attitudes and way of life to the lower reaches of the peerage, and it is with them, or with the leading elements among them, that social and matrimonial ties were maintained.

Within very broad limits, and admitting many individual exceptions to the rule, the hierarchy of ranks corresponded very roughly to categories of income, though unfortunately for the historian anomalies are too numerous to allow the generalization to be applied to individuals without careful investigation of the particular circumstances. Contemporaries certainly thought that gradations of title meant, on an average, gradations of wealth. This is accepted by Thomas Wilson at the beginning of the seventeenth century and by a much shrewder student of the social structure, Gregory King, at the end. The hypothesis is also

[3] A. H. Smith, *The Elizabethan Gentry of Norfolk* (London Ph.D. thesis, 1959), pp. 3–5. A. M. Everett, *The County Committee of Kent in the Civil War*, Leicester, 1957, p. 8.

supported by an admittedly crude and unsatisfactory calculation of the declared wealth of Royalist peers and baronets in 1642.[4] Moreover, the very survival of these titular rankings as an important element in English society and politics well into the nineteenth century also suggests that they bore some relation to economic realities. For in the long run, if the hierarchy of titles does not bear a fairly close relation to the hierarchy of wealth, the system of stratification will sooner or later be discredited and overthrown. A condition of the survival of any system is either that society is static, with no new wealth being acquired except by the privileged classes, or else that money, from however tainted a source, is permitted to purchase status. Only if he is certain that his son, if not himself, will enjoy the position and respect commensurate with his wealth, will the self-made man be content to accept the built-in rigidities of the stratification system as he finds it. It has been the readiness of the landed classes to accept on equal terms wealth from any source at one generation's remove which has given the English social framework its remarkable stability, despite the huge turnover of pedigreed families and the growing volume of new wealth from non-landed sources.

The Peerage

The titular peerage formed the top layer or layers of this hierarchical, pyramidal structure. In the eyes of the sixteenth century, they were a distinct group of the nobility, *nobilitas maior,* as distinct from the *nobilitas minor* of knights, esquires, and armigerous gentry; the one was the flower, the other the root, said Richard Mulcaster in 1581. The criterion of an English peer of the realm was the right to sit in the House of Lords, a right obtained either by letters patent or by receipt of a writ of summons. The only difference between the two was that the former descended with the tail male, and the latter with the heirs general. Since in the sixteenth century most peers were created by patent, male succession took on an increased importance. Already in the fourteenth century writs of summons were issued not in respect of legal tenure, but of wealth and political influence, the tenurial barony being ancient, vague and outdated.[5] By the end of the

    [4] C. B. Macpherson, *The Political Theory of Possessive Individualism,* Oxford, 1962, p. 280. E. C. Klotz and G. Davies, 'The Wealth of Royalist Peers and Baronets', *EHR,* lviii, 1943.
    [5] S. Painter, *Studies in the History of the English Feudal Barony,* Baltimore, 1943, pp. 54–55. Mulcaster, op. cit., p. 200.

fifteenth century it was the usual, but by no means inevitable, practice
to summon all who had previously received a writ, unless they were
attainted or under age or or otherwise incapacitated. Those who could
no longer maintain status because of poverty were quietly dropped
from the list. George Neville, Duke of Bedford, disappeared in 1478,
the Marquis of Berkeley in 1492. If and when wealth once more came
their way, however, they again took their rightful place. Thus the lords
Clinton dropped out from 1460 to 1514, and the earls of Kent from
1523 until summoned again by Elizabeth in 1572. But during the
sixteenth century the legal definition hardened on the basis of an in-
alienable hereditary right. By the reign of Elizabeth ambiguities and
uncertainties had been ironed out and there was no longer much serious
doubt about who was, and who was not, a peer of the realm. The legal
position was now clear.

With the bare title went a number of privileges, legal, financial,
and political, which distinguished the aristocracy from the lesser nobility below them. They were favoured before the law in that they could
not be arrested except for treason, felony, or breach of the peace, a
matter of considerable importance at a time when this was a favourite
weapon in the armoury of the balked creditor. They could not be out-
lawed, they were free of various writs designed to force men to appear
in court, they were not obliged to testify under oath. In consequence
they were very slippery customers to catch in the tattered net of the
contemporary common law procedure. In criminal actions they had to
be tried before their peers rather than before a common jury. This last
in fact had little practical value, since if the Crown brought an action
for treason or felony against a peer, the result was all but a foregone
conclusion, whatever the social complexion of the jury. Whenever they
were asked to do so, the Lords nearly always obediently convicted the
royal victim (the sole notable exception being the acquittal of Lord
Dacre in 1534). The only protection their rank afforded them here was
that their bodies were safe from torture in life and dismemberment
after death.

They were also free from many of the burdens of local government.
They did not sit on juries, could not be picked as sheriffs, and were
not obliged to turn up at county musters. Their military obligations
were assessed not by the local authorities but by six fellow-peers, and
their liability to tax was assessed by commissioners working directly
under the Lord Chancellor and the Lord Treasurer. The country as a
whole was assessed regionally by local commissioners, but after 1523

peers were exempted from the humiliation of having to conform to the decisions of mere squires and gentry. Though there was a very sharp fall in the assessment of peers in the late sixteenth century, it is not yet certain that this exceeded the general trend towards under-assessment of the propertied classes. Here again, therefore, the difference was one of form rather than of substance.

Hereditary noblemen could in fact, though not in theory, rely on most if not all high offices in the royal household, some embassies, some military commands and most Lord Lieutenantcies being reserved for them to the exclusion of mere commoners. Indeed by the reign of Charles I the peerage had achieved almost a complete monopoly of this last office, twenty-nine out of the thirty-three holders being earls or their heirs male, the remainder being made up of two viscounts, one baron, and a bishop. But they could lay no claims to any of the greater offices of state, like Lord Treasurer or Lord Chancellor, nor to any fixed proportion of seats on the Privy Council. Holders of high political office were usually given titles to increase the respect accorded to them and to their office, and some important offices were always given to old aristocratic families to secure their support and strengthen their loyalty, but hereditary claims as such were never recognized by either the Tudors or the Early Stuarts.

Finally the peers sat apart, along with the bishops, in one of the two representative assemblies of the kingdom which together, and in conjunction with the King, made up Parliament. Owing to a concentration of modern research upon the lower house, the great power exercised by the Lords in Tudor legislation is in danger of being seriously underestimated. Within this body the importance of lay peers was greatly increased first by the disappearance of the abbots at the Dissolution of the Monasteries, and then by the collapse of the prestige and social standing of the bishops. After 1560 the Upper House was dominated and controlled by the lay peers, the bishops having already taken up their now familiar role of obsequious yes-men for the current ruling clique. Moreover, since peers, unlike commoners, were entitled to vote by proxy, even the aged or infirm who could not stand the journey to London were able to influence decisions by entrusting their proxy to a friend of similar outlook. Looked at as a power *élite* they consistently filled high political office, they occupied at least half the seats in the Privy Council (if only thanks to concurrent elevation to a title), they formed one of the two legislative bodies in Parliament, they had a near monopoly of the Lord-Lieutenantcies, and they were

in a position to exercise great influence on county politics and administration by virtue of their territorial holdings and their train of clients.
It was the peerage who stole the limelight in the Tudor political system,
even if it was the gentry whose interests ultimately prevailed. If the
gentry were the ruling, the aristocracy were the governing class.

The significance of these privileges and distinctions should not be
over-emphasized. They conferred certain benefits, and served to mark
the peerage off from the rest of the community, but they were of limited
economic or legal importance. The immunities before the law were
helpful rather than decisive, and no one waxed rich merely by being
in a position to bilk creditors or evade parliamentary taxes. This is in
striking contrast with the situation on the Continent, where a title of
nobility conferred favours so enormous as to cut their holders off from
the rest of the community upon the fruit of whose labours they existed.
English historians in the Whig tradition have in consequence been
inclined to picture this country as one with a long history as an open
society. This is an oversimplification. Social stratification was very rigid
indeed in seventeenth-century England, and mobility from the lower
levels into the upper gentlemanly bracket, which had been so common
half a century before, was becoming increasingly difficult by 1640.
Legal and fiscal inequalities existed, privilege was King. Those who
belittle these facts, who pretend that seventeenth-century England was
a land of free opportunity, who profess to be unable to distinguish
between a gentleman and a baronet, a baronet and an earl, betray their
insensitivity to the basic presuppositions of Stuart society.

On the other hand, it is equally misleading to claim that English
society was virtually indistinguishable from that which flourished on
the continent of Europe before the French Revolution. The permeation
of eighteenth-century society by merchant wealth, the orientation of
late seventeenth- and eighteenth-century foreign policy towards the
promotion of economic interests, the influence in the House of Commons of the East Indies or the West Indies interest, the heavy burden
of taxation borne by the landed nobility, the importance of joint stock
investments and the Bank of England, the relative freedom from personal oppression and economic misery of the peasantry, all point to the
fact that there were striking differences between the two societies.

The titular peerage, then, was a status group defined by special
privileges of its own, and the major component of a power *élite*. But
was it anything more than that? Was it a class, in the narrow sense of
the word, a body of men with similar economic interests, enjoying sim-

ilar incomes derived from similar sources? There can be no doubt that
landed income was a basic criterion of title. Edward Chamberlayne
explained in 1669 that 'The Laws and Customs of England . . . expected that each of [the Degrees of Honour] should have a convenient
Estate and Value of Lands of Inheritance, for the support of their
Honours and the Kings Service'. As we have seen, after the middle of
the sixteenth century, impoverished peers ceased to be excluded from
the House of Lords. One result of the boarding up of this convenient
drop-hatch for the indigent was the development of a potential discrepancy between wealth and title. This was why in 1629 the House
of Lords petitioned the King to give the Earl of Oxford an estate, so
that he could support his dignity. Failing royal aid—and it usually did
fail—the only solution was to trade title for money in marriage with
an heiress. On the other hand, it continued to be widely accepted that
wealth was an essential qualification for the aspiring social climber.
Burghley's list of candidates for the peerage in 1588 was headed
'Knightes of great possessions'; and the financial basis of titular status
was openly recognized by the practice of selling peerages, baronetages,
and knighthoods. Buckingham was attacked in the Commons for giving
peerages to poor relations, and Oliver Cromwell was similarly reproved
thirty years later. 'It is estates that make men Lords and esteemed in
the country', he was told.[6] Despite these backsliders from the conven-
tions of the day, entry into the higher status groups continued to be
directly related to wealth—and landed wealth at that. The result was
that on the average and without prejudice to individual exceptions,
legal status remained a reasonably close indicator of financial means.

On the other hand, it would foolish to deny that there was a
considerable 'looseness', as Talcott Parsons would call it, between the
cream of the gentry—the handful of leading county families—and the
lower ranks of the peerage. There were 121 peerage families in 1641
and there were probably another 30 to 40 upper gentry families who
were as rich as the middling barons and richer than the poor ones.
There were some very wealthy families like the Pastons or the Thynnes
who for one reason or another refused or were not offered a title, there
were some new peers who were never rich, like Boteler or Mohun or
Savile, and there were some old peers who had become poor, like Vaux
or Stourton or Windsor.

If we regard the gentry *élite* and the titular peerage as forming a

[6] J. Rushworth, *Historical Collections*, i, p. 339. J. Firth, *House of Lords in
the Great Civil War*, 1910, p. 257.

single class, we can see that it is defined in a number of ways. In the first place, its members stood out because of their wealth. As a result of this wealth, they lived in a more opulent style than their neighbours with more servants, more horses, more coaches, and a more open table. They occupied a larger house, built on the court-yard or E plan, rather than that of the 'double-pile' favoured by those of lesser means. They were often educated by private tutors, they were fellow commoners at the university, and they rounded off their adolescence with the Grand Tour. They mostly married among themselves. They or their sons controlled or filled the county seats in Parliament. They were bound by the same moral pressure to spend freely, to serve the State, and to treat their tenants well. Whatever may be said of the earls, therefore, the baronage at any given time only represents the majority of the greater landowners of the country. Although for some purposes the lives of this non-noble gentry *élite* are freely drawn upon for illustrative material, the statistical skeleton of this book [*The Crisis of The Aristocracy, 1540–1640*, from which this selection has been taken] is the titular peerage. This is a defensible procedure since the peerage, embracing as it does about two-thirds of the total families in this economic class— and all those in the really very high income bracket—may fairly be taken as a representative selection.

There is no doubt, however, that the representative value of the peerage changes over the eighty years from 1560 to 1640. A reasonable majority grouping of the greater landowners in 1560, by 1600 there was urgent need to admit new blood to maintain the close relationship of title to landed wealth. This was achieved by James in 1603, but the massive inflation of the peerage under the Duke of Buckingham introduced new elements of uncertainty. A number of the new arrivals lacked the financial backing needed to maintain the position of a baron, while by now some members of the older aristocracy had fallen upon hard times. Moreover, there had been admitted one or two rich merchants. Although these men had conscientiously shifted their wealth from trade into broad acres and a country seat, they were nevertheless too fresh from the counting-house to have had time to wash their hands. At the same time the way of life of the older aristocracy had undergone a sea-change. No longer interested in manpower, they had begun to exploit more fully the financial possibilities of their estates, they had abandoned the rigours of military service, they had migrated from the country to the Court, they had reduced their households and cut down on the excesses of rural hospitality, they had turned eagerly to joint stock adventures, urban development, and mining speculations. The peerage in 1640 was a landed aristocracy increasingly devoted to money-making, infiltrated partly by a capitalist bourgeoisie obsessed with aristocratic pretensions, and partly by jumped-up lesser gentry who owed their elevation to political favour but some of whom had failed to extract from the Crown the favour of a great landed estate with which to endow their successors. Unattractive though it may be to those with romantic illusions about rank and title, it has been the successful fusion of old blood, new wealth, and political careerism that has given the English peerage its remarkable capacity for survival over the past three centuries.

If the titular peerage was a status group and if together with a further thirty or forty families it formed a single economic class, it remains true nevertheless that there were both marked internal gradations and important differences between the numerous variables in ranking which together formed the social stratification system. Within the peerage, dukes, marquises, and earls were in economic resources, political influence, and social prestige set somewhat apart from viscounts and barons. The significance of this division is shown by the fact that when titles were offered for sale by James, it cost just as much to rise from a baron to an earl as from a gentleman to a baron. The wealth of earls and above was on the average much greater than that of viscounts and below, the Royalist Composition papers suggesting that in 1642 it averaged as much as double. With this far greater wealth went a distinctly superior style of living, far greater territorial influence, and a claim to offices at Court to which no mere barons could reasonably aspire simply by virtue of their titles. Here, therefore, is a rift of some importance in the ranks of the peerage, which it will be necessary to emphasize from time to time if a misleading impression of homogeneity is not to be created.

Another obvious division was that of birth, between great families of several generations' standing and those but newly risen to wealth and dignity. At all periods men of inherited position have tended to forget the humble and often sordid origins of their family greatness, and have looked with distaste upon the rise of new men to their own degree of eminence.

BIBLIOGRAPHY

Mildred Campbell, *The English Yeoman Under Elizabeth and the Early Stuarts*, New Haven, 1942.

Ruth Kelso, *The Doctrine of the English Gentleman in the Sixteenth Century*, University of Illinois Studies in Language and Literature, Vol. 14, Nos. 1–2, 1929.

Roland Mousnier, *La Vénalité des Offices sous Henri IV et Louis XIII*, Paris, 1945.

A. S. Turberville, *The House of Lords in the Reign of William III*, Oxford, 1913.

ENTREPRENEURIAL ACTIVITIES OF THE SWEDISH ARISTOCRACY *

Goran Ohlin

In the Introduction to the previous essay, we said that there were no basic dissimilarities between the class structure of England in the sixteenth and seventeenth centuries and those of other European countries but that, nevertheless, there were subtle differences which were, in certain contexts, very important. Here we have an example. Attitudes and activities of the aristocracy of birth in the area of commerce and industry were somewhat different in different countries, and this had important social consequences for these various places. In Sweden, and in England too, aristocratic attitudes were a little more favorable, and activities somewhat larger, in regard to business than were those of their counterparts in, say, France or Spain. Ohlin's essay is a valuable account of this subject, and it has the added virtue of providing us with a comparative view of a country which is often not given its due share of attention in general books on European history. Here again, also, we learn about mobility into and out of the presumably hereditary and fixed nobility.

Goran Ohlin is a Swedish economic historian who has taught at Harvard and Columbia. He is now a member of the Wenner-Gren Institute in Stockholm.

In recent attempts at formulating the relationships between social structure and economic development, the transition from pro-capitalistic

---

* Reprinted from *Explorations in Entrepreneurial History*, 6 (1954), 147–162. Reprinted by permission of the author.

and pre-industrial society to high capitalism has sometimes been described as a change from a state in which personal relationships are "functionally diffuse" and "particularistic" to one where they are "functionally specific" and "universalistic," from a system of "ascribed" to one of "achieved" status.[1] This formula goes back to such sociological theories as Sir Henry Maine's "movement from status to contract" and Tönnies's *Gemeinschaft und Gesellschaft*. Applied to the history of the West, the formula would seem to imply that the institution of hereditary aristocracy must be more or less incompatible with modern capitalism, or at any rate be a "dysfunctional" element. But structural-functional analysis in this simple form is based on ideal types, namely those of "initial" and "resultant" stages, and consequently does not mirror the process of historical change in all its fullness.

The choice of stages is, of course, a matter of heuristic expediency, but if the Middle Ages are chosen as a pre-capitalistic initial stage, and the late nineteenth century as a resultant stage characterized by reasonably well-developed capitalistic institutions, the whole period of modern history appears as a stage of transition. This point of view implies the existence of continuous change. When we analyze the process of change, we must distinguish between the readiness and responsiveness of the social environment on the one hand, and the origin of change on the other. It is, for instance, entirely possible that a social system which recruits its elite in a way which seems to constitute a barrier to economic development may nevertheless receive important impulses to innovation from its elite. Whether or not the nobility of the West played a role in providing such impulses is certainly a relevant question.

Traditionally, economic history has not emphasized the contribution of the nobility to European economic development. To be sure, there have been minor exceptions. The importance of the enclosures, for which the English aristocracy was responsible, has always been recognized; and Sombart has expressly pointed to the entrepreneurial activities of the European aristocracy. Schumpeter's thinking may seem to link aristocracy and entrepreneurship, but it is aristocracy in the broad sense of an elite with which he is concerned. American historians usually overestimate early commerce as the breeding ground for modern entrepreneurship, while Max Weber and Sombart rather stressed the role of dissenters and aliens, such as Puritans and Jews.

As a matter of fact, in Europe the traditional value systems of most

[1] As those terms are used by, e.g., Parsons, Linton, and Levy.

national aristocracies did not encourage business activities. But innovational entrepreneurship is in any case a matter of deviance, and if a European aristocrat deviated from his traditional social role by engaging in commerce and industry, he was likely to be less prone to humdrum routine than the merchant of lowlier estate. And there are still other reasons why we might expect to find at least potential entrepreneurs among the members of the nobility: the possession, at times, of great wealth; the need for large incomes to finance required or extravagant consumption; a status sufficiently elevated and secure to allow for eccentricities, including industrial experimentation; international contacts making for the transmission of new ideas; and education, on occasion, which amounted to a liberation from the shackles of mercantile tradition, if a nobleman actually went into business.

Conversely, an inquiry into the contribution of various national aristocracies to economic development is also bound to raise the problem of how economic development brought about changes in the composition of those aristocracies. Noble status was never merely hereditary. A study of nobility must, ipso facto, involve a study of social mobility. The origins, orientation, exclusiveness, and so forth of the European nobility varied from time to time and from place to place. Whether the recruitment of any national aristocracy was influenced by economic development may be said to be a secondary research problem, derived from the primary study of the influence of the nobility on economic development. But there was, of course, genuine interaction. At all events, the nature and origin of social elites are sociological problems of first rank and are likely to be closely interrelated with the question of their contribution to change. The different degree of flexibility of the elites in various countries is certainly an important variable.[2]

I

All over Europe, monarchic and aristocratic institutions were essentially alike, especially with regard to behavior patterns, forms, and com-

---

[2] For a general historico-sociological discussion of the role of various aristocracies, see the series of articles in *Annales d'histoire économique et sociale*, 1936–1937, especially Marc Bloch, "Sur le passé de la noblesse française; quelque jalons de recherche," *ibid.*, VIII (1936), p. 366; Gino Luzzato, "Les activités économiques du patriciat vénitien," *ibid.*, IX 1937), p. 25; T. H. Marshall, "L'aristocratie britannique de nos jours," *ibid.* IX (1937), p. 236. Also, with numerous references to the economic activities of the Belgian and French aristocracy: Robert J. Lamoine, "Classes sociales et attitudes révolutionnaires: quelque reflexions sur un chapitre d'histoire belge," *ibid.*, VII (1935), p. 160.

munity of interests. Yet, economically, legally, and politically, there were considerable differences from country to country. The economic activities of the Swedish aristocracy must, therefore, be presented against the background of its general characteristics.

In medieval Sweden "noble" title could be claimed by anyone who was ready to serve his king as a mounted warrior or who provided such a warrior. Military service appeared as the commutation of a fiscal obligation, so that nobles were exempt from taxes. Strictly speaking, noble status (*frälse*) was neither permanent nor hereditary; as it was open to everybody who assumed its burdens, so everybody who so preferred could renounce it and resume payment of the land tax. Thus title and status were tied to land; landed wealth was not only a prerequisite for the service in question, but the whole institution of nobility rested in theory on the conversion of the land tax.

Toward the end of the Middle Ages, the political power of this aristocracy was supreme. The elected kings were its puppets. Economically, however, even the very considerable properties of the wealthier nobles were not administered by the owners. Absentee landlords, they collected rents from relatively independent peasants who cultivated their holdings under village self-government. The nobles constituted a military and political elite, consisting of probably less than one hundred families all told, and drawing its strength from inherited landed property.

In a momentous period of Swedish history, royal power was asserted by Gustavus Vasa (*regnabat* 1520–1560) and the hereditary monarchy established. Politically, this meant the end of aristocratic rule, a change which led to the emergence of a new conception of the function of the nobility. Under Gustavus Vasa the Swedish nation obtained a political organization of unprecedented strength, and the public administration created for the implementation of royal economic and social policies was in need of personnel. Thus to the military function of the nobility was added that of civil service. Its obligation to serve the state was emphasized in the patents, privileges, and charters issued to those ennobled in the sixteenth century, while Swedish noble status, like the monarchy, was made hereditary. Soon administrative duties of various kinds became far more important for certain noblemen than military service, and in the end the latter was no longer even a prerequisite for knighthood. In 1569 it was ruled that nobles whose landholdings were too small to provide a mounted warrior could sell their estates and still retain their status. If, on the other hand, they later acquired land again, they had to resume their military obligations. Landless noblemen were allowed to move to the cities and engage in trade. The landed nobility, on the other hand, was limited in its economic freedom because of the prevailing public policy which restricted trade to the confines of the cities and prevented so-called rural trading. But an important exception was made: noblemen were allowed to sell their own produce and purchase commodities, at home or abroad, for their own consumption, provided that they did not encroach upon the privileges of the town merchants. . . .

II

From a study of the composition in the eighteenth century of the Swedish House of Lords (which included the untitled nobility), it is possible to give some figures reflecting the "occupational structure" of the nobility at that time:

	1718/19		1765/66	
Officers	2,279	72.5%	2,367	73.3%
Civil servants	403	12.8	462	14.3
Courtiers	32	1.0	210	6.5
Clergymen	7	0.2	10	0.3
Ironmasters & Copper Smelters	19	0.6	27	0.8
Minors (no occ.)	293	9.3	Not listed	
Miscellaneous	117	3.6	153	4.8
Total	3,145	100.0	3,229	100.0

As this table shows, there were few nobles even in the eighteenth century for whom industry or trade could be said to be a main pursuit. Typically the nobleman was a soldier, a statesman, or at least a public administrator. The emphasis on these pursuits was strong enough to cause comment by a foreign student of the Swedish scene, the Italian nobleman Allessandro Bichi, who remarked on the pride of the Swedish nobility: "It devotes itself neither to the Church, nor to the sciences, not even to professions like medicine; it consents to serve only in the government of the country or in the military, of which the latter suits them better than politics."

Thus one is not very likely to find a great many professional merchants or industrialists among the nobility—except, of course, those who had attained their status on the strength of success in business. In those cases there arises the interesting problem of the second generation. Nevertheless, there were within the nobles' traditional sphere of interest a number of fields of potential entrepreneurial activity. Tentatively one might indicate the following areas in which economic decisions of an entrepreneurial nature might be taken by a nobleman:

1. First of all, their land-holdings put the nobility in a strategic economic position. The development of *Gutsherrschaft* came very late in Sweden, as will appear in later discussion. Yet, however restricted the nobility's interest in agricultural management, potentially there was a field for innovation in agricultural technique as well as in trade in agricultural products.

2. The necessity of disposing of their agricultural surplus forced the nobility into trade; incidentally, before the emergence of a money economy, this was no less true of all other recipients of rent. The government, receiving its taxes in kind, was also driven into trade on a considerable scale. Market-oriented activities of this kind on the part of government servants, recruited from the nobility, would seem to deserve attention.

Payments in kind were late in disappearing from the Swedish scene, but even after the final introduction of a money economy, government service remained a field for entrepreneurial activity by noblemen-entrepreneurs, as everywhere else in the Mercantilist period.

3. The military organization absorbed, as we have seen, the majority of the nobles. Glory had its price, and the economic aspects of warfare were of vast significance. Before the bureaucratization of the services, a variety of strictly economic duties rested upon Swedish higher officers. Related to the development of the military arts was that of the munitions industries and of the trade in military supplies, in which noblemen participated.

4. Private industrial activity, profit-oriented and unrelated to government, might be expected as an adjunct to agriculture, as a side-line of higher civil servants in possession of vital inside information, or among noblemen in search of profitable investment of their wealth.

With such tentative ideas, we might set out to survey the role of the nobility in Swedish economic development up to the moment when in the eighteenth century *l'ancien regime* began to disintegrate.

III

In spite of the immense land-holdings of the nobility in the late Middle Ages and the sixteenth century, large-scale agriculture was exceptional. The bulk of the nobility's holdings, as well as those of the Crown, were tenancies, and the "manors" were few and relatively insignificant. . . .

Ever since 1284 rural trading had been forbidden in Sweden, in an attempt to reserve trade for the city merchants, but from this regulation was exempted the exchange of a man's own products for "arms, cloth, linen, salt, hops or whatever else he might need for his own use." In such trade, the nobility, besides other smaller producers, took a large part, and the export books of Stockholm, which have been preserved, list as exporters members of the royal family and the peerage. However, the nobility often ventured into large-scale trade, far beyond the exchange of its own products. . . .

Of all the noble traders in commodities received by way of taxation or rent payment in sixteenth century Sweden, the one who has attracted the most attention was the King himself, namely Gustavus Vasa, often called the country's greatest businessman of his time. The source material is excellent on this point, and may produce a temptation to overrate the importance of his entrepreneurial activities. But undoubtedly the King's trade in grain, butter, oxen, iron, and other commodities was the best organized of any in the country; in this field as in his never-ending concern with industry, especially with the iron industry, Gustavus Vasa reveals his exceptional entrepreneurial talent. Keeping close watch over prices and supplies, he transported products, paid to the Crown as revenue, from surplus to deficit areas, striking good bargains and stabilizing the food situation in different parts of the country. His conception of the economy remained medieval, but he wrested the country from the control of the Hansards, who had regarded it as a field for colonial exploitation. He promoted its industries by State enterprise as well as by education of the Swedes, for whose business acumen he had the utmost contempt, and in so doing he relied heavily on foreigners, especially Germans. . . .

IV

For Sweden, the seventeenth century was a period of military and political expansion and exertion. In economic matters, the country's development was drastically accelerated by the exposure of her leading citizens to foreign examples and by the unprecedented influx of foreigners in the Swedish armies and above all in business and politics. It was a development which bore the imprint not only of technological and ideological diffusion and imitation, but also of the war effort into which the country's resources were channeled so far as the rigidity of a preeminently agricultural economy permitted. . . .

Within the ranks of the old aristocracy we find represented all the kinds of economic activity previously suggested. In the first place, the agricultural holdings of the nobility were considerably enlarged, primarily as the result of donations of the state land in return for military and political service. In fact, the land grant was one of the common ways of achieving a settlement when the Crown was in arrears with the salaries of its officers. . . .

Secondly, among the economic privileges which the nobility enjoyed, the exemption from duties on foreign and domestic trade was the most hotly contested, especially when it was applied not merely to the nobles' own products and household needs. Throughout the century the delegates of the townsmen continued their complaints about noble competition and indeed about the very right of the nobility to trade at all. . . .

An interest in trade was also demonstrated by the investments of some members of the aristocracy who contributed to the financing of the various trading companies of the time—the Oxenstierna family, for example, held shares in the African Company, besides participating in numerous shipping ventures.

Trade in grain was commonly at the root of the nobility's commercial ventures. This grain was usually sold to domestic or foreign merchants, but another pattern evolved in addition which deserves some attention. Grain was directly or indirectly exchanged for copper from the Falun mines, and the metal was then exported on behalf of the nobles. . . .

Opposition to the nobility's ventures into business was not limited to competing tradesmen. In the field of mining and metallurgy it was the policy of the government to keep the production of ores and metal out of the hands of noblemen, in spite of the existence of an old-established fiscal privilege for nobles working the ore on their own land; as early as 1485 it had been stipulated that nobles should be exempt from taxes on metal so produced, whereas commoners had to pay a duty of one-tenth of their output. Noble rights in this field persisted in the seventeenth century, although nobles were then forced to pay a tax of one-thirtieth. . . .

As a rule, the Crown's iron mines and iron works were not sold but leased to private operators, and in this way prominent nobles—often military men and civil servants—entered the industry. The part played by the mercantile nobility already mentioned was perhaps more spectacular; men like Louis de Geer and the de Besches attained leadership in the iron industry as in other fields. . . .

V

To the old nobility, public regulation of the metal industries, as well as of commerce and industry in general, offered perhaps a richer field for entrepreneurial activity than management in their own behalf. To safeguard the national interest in the efficient operation of the mines and metal works, Crown-owned and private alike, Gustavus Adolphus in 1630 established the so-called *Bergsamt,* a government agency which was to supervise the entire industry and to study carefully the profitability and production record of each and every mine in the country. In 1637 it was reorganized and named the *Generalbergsamt,* the first president of which was Carl Bonde, a member of one of the oldest families of rank and a highly capable administrator. Bonde was one of the originators of the idea that the Swedish iron industry should be merged into a national cartel, in order to exploit the prominent position enjoyed by Swedish iron in foreign markets. In 1625 an attempt was made to set up an Iron Company for this purpose. The attempt failed, but the plan was gradually realized by the extension of state control to the point where a reasonably efficient cartel had been established for iron exports. Production quotas were set and enforced with what was for the time amazing administrative success. In 1649 the *Generalbergsamt* was reorganized and its status again raised; the result was the *Kungl.* (Royal) *Bergskollegium,* the head of which, with the title of governor, was to be a member of the Lord Council, and whose six secretaries (*assessorer*) were to be of noble rank.

The government's active and supervisory interest in the economy extended far beyond the metal industries. In all industries closely affecting the national interest the government appointed factors or supervisors.

One Johan Månsson Ulfsparre was appointed supervisor of the country's saltpetre plants by Gustavus Adolphus. On another occasion the position is reported to have been filled by Åke Axelsson Natt och Dag, like Ulfsparre a nobleman of high rank. Erik Larsson, a foreigner raised to nobility under the name of von der Linde, and Louis de Geer, whom we meet here for the second time, were made "factors" in the salt trade, and the Crown also encouraged, operated, or leased soap pans, paper mills, sugar refineries, powder mills, and so on, especially in the decades before 1650. As diplomatic envoys, noblemen were forced to concern themselves with the promotion of trade. Thus in 1634 a Swedish delegation consisting of several prominent nobles and one merchant was despatched to Russia and Persia for negotiations—rather futile ones, as it turned out—about the opening of an easterly trade route via Sweden's trans-Baltic provinces and Russia to Persia.

The strategic copper exports represented one, but only one, area in which the government stood in need of commercial and financial expertise rarely possessed by the old Swedish aristocracy, and to a large extent relied on competent foreigners. The imports of military supplies and the arrangement of foreign credit was another field of activity for this group, as well as the organization of Swedish munitions manufacture. Iron works, cannon forges, and ordnance factories mushroomed under the guidance of these immigrants.

The military remained, of course, the foremost vocation of the aristocracy. After the reorganization of the military service carried out by Gustavus Vasa little scope was left for Swedish military entrepreneurship, especially since the Swedish army consisted mostly of mercenary troops. To be sure, traces can be found; the career of Jacob de la Gardie (1583–1652) provides an excellent example. Moreover in 1629 it was ordered that a certain percentage of the soldiers' pay was to be handed over to their captains or colonels for the purchase of weapons, but this system, elsewhere part and parcel of military entrepreneurship, was quickly abandoned. When later in the Thirty Years' War, after the death of Gustavus Adolphus, Sweden came to rely on mercenaries, military entrepreneurship was provided by German rather than Swedish officers and noblemen.

It could probably be said, however, that the strongest entrepreneurial impulses affecting the Swedish officer class stemmed from the practice of substituting land grants for cash payments. This system prevailed in the army as well as in the navy. Naval officers were in some cases paid by privileges which resulted in or promoted entrepreneurial activities. One major Taring Henriksson, for example, was permitted the use of one of the navy's ships for a trade expedition of his own to Portugal. And again, one Captain Hans Bengtsson Menig, who had resigned in 1660 to become a merchant skipper, arrived in Stockholm in 1666 with a cargo of salt and was granted exemption from the duty to the amount of his unpaid salary.

Apart from its contribution to the regulation and management of the semi-public mining and metal industry, the nobility has a hand in a great many other commercial and industrial enterprises. Some of these were related to the war effort, as for instance alum, saltpetre, and gunpowder plants and textile mills established by members of the nobility.

In this connection we encounter a remarkable female entrepreneur of noble origin, the Countess Marie Sophie Oxenstierna, née de la Gardie (1627–1694). Already mentioned as an exporter of timber, the Countess also exported grain, potash and wool, and invested in trading companies. She operated textile, paper and powder mills in the vicinity of her chateau at Tyresö, as well as several lighthouses on the coast. By 1670 the output of her textile mills was supposed to have amounted to 30,000 yards of cloth per year. In 1667, becoming a creative entrepreneur, she opened the first coal mines in Sweden, supplying her lighthouses with some of the coal and exporting the remainder.

In a large number of cases, wealthy landlords also established brick and glass-making plants of local significance. More importantly, the first half of the seventeenth century saw the creation of a multitude of chartered companies, many of them trading companies modeled on Dutch examples. Such were the South Sea Company (1649), the New Sweden Company (1637), and the African Company (1649), all founded for the implementation of ambitious colonization schemes of which New Sweden in Delaware was the only one which met with any success worth mentioning. Of more importance were the chartered companies in fields like copper, tar, tobacco, salt, and sugar, all aiming at profitable foreign trade under protection of monopoly rights. The management of such corporations was largely in the hands of those enterprising foreigners who have so frequently been mentioned. The old nobility, however, participated along with non-noble civil servants as investors in most of those projects. Axel Oxenstierna and his sons were partners in the African Company, and hardly a family in the high aristocracy is not mentioned as a shareholder in one corporation or another.

It is questionable, however, whether investments by nobles in such ventures were large. As Heckscher points out, the Swedish aristocrats were not renowned for their thrift. When the first Swedish bank was established, only a few members of the aristocracy appeared as depositors. It was as borrowers that the nobles availed themselves of the services of the bank, and almost every family of the old aristocracy is found in the list.

VI

In general, Swedish nobles did not enjoy too favorable a reputation as businessmen. The illustrious industrialist and financier, Louis de

Geer, who had moved to Sweden from Holland, was said occasionally to sigh, "Swedes will be Swedes." And he seems to have had good cause. When, for instance, he was trying to recover a debt from Gustaf Leijon-hufvud, he was told that it was "unheard of among honest men of noble blood that one would make cause against the other over such a trifle." Another Swedish noble found the foreigners' insistence on precision in affairs rather a burden: Johan Skytte complained that the Dutch were so "curiosi in rebus minimis." And abroad, even Savary warned: "Il faut remarquer qu'a Stokolm les debiteurs ne peuvent estre contrains en payement de ce qu'ils doivent par aucune rigeur, c'est pourquoi l'on doit plustost se faire tirer que d'y remettre."

BIBLIOGRAPHY

P. E. Fahlbeck, "La Noblesse de Suède: Etude Démographique," *Bulletin de l'institut international de statistique,* XII (1900), 169–181.

Charles A. Foster, *Honoring Commerce and Industry in 18th Century France: a Case Study of Changes in Traditional Social Functions,* Unpublished Ph.D. Dissertation, Harvard University, 1950.

Henri Lévy-Bruhl, "La noblesse de France et le commerce à la fin de l'ancien régime," *Revue d'histoire moderne,* VIII (1923), 211ff.

Lawrence Stone, "The Nobility in Business, 1540–1640," *Explorations in Entrepreneurial History,* X (1957), 54–61.

THE MYTH OF THE MIDDLE CLASS
IN TUDOR ENGLAND *

J. H. Hexter

The notion of "the rising middle class" has been a cover for social ideology and intellectual confusion alike. Hexter here brilliantly exposes both ideology and confusion in order to set the record straight, to show that while there was a good deal of individual mobility into and up out of the bourgeoisie or middle class in seventeenth century England, this

* Reprinted from *Explorations in Entrepreneurial History,* II (1950), 128–140. A much extended and completely documented version of this essay can be found in J. H. Hexter, *Reappraisals in History,* Northwestern University Press. 1961; published in England by Longmans, Green & Co., Limited, 1961.

class itself does not seem to have been increasing in relative size or in power or in self-consciousness or in aspiration to rule. Moreover, it is clear that rising middle class individuals thought of themselves as aspirant nobility, not as members of a revolutionary and corporate group. They accepted the established class structure; they were not out to change it.

Perhaps the moral may also be drawn from Hexter's essay that historical analysis can move from what he calls "elegant fictions" to accounts that are closer to social reality. Such successive approximations to social reality validate the claim that some make for history that it can be, in part, a social science.

J. H. Hexter, who has taught at Queens College, New York, and Washington University, St. Louis, has recently joined the History Department at Yale University. He has written not only about the social and intellectual history of Tudor and Stuart England but about European intellectual figures such as Machiavelli and Sir Thomas More.

The Tudors were especially favorable "to commerce and the middle classes on which the new monarchy rested." They "attached themselves to the rising commercial classes." This is the myth of the middle class in Tudor England. Although the myth itself is considerably older, that part of it dealing with the Tudor period became orthodox historical dogma only forty years ago, when Professor Pollard pronounced its authenticity in *Factors in Modern History*. His essay on "The Advent of the Middle Class" attributed to this ostensibly omnipotent group every significant phenomenon in European and especially in English history for three centuries—the Renaissance, the Reformation, the colonial expansion of Europe, the New Monarchy, nationalism, the rise of the House of Commons, the Puritan Revolution. His conclusions have won almost universal acceptance. With but few exceptions the roster of those following Pollard's lead includes every distinguished historian who has discussed Tudor history in the past forty years, and a legion of undistinguished ones.

So we have on our hands a full-blown myth, which by explaining everything has come to emanate an aura of sacredness, of mystical untouchability. To doubt it smacks of heresy, blasphemy and sacrilege.

Now to make a shambles of a myth is not always necessarily desirable, for myths may serve as a vigorous stimulus to intellectual as well as to social effort. There is, however, a point hard to define when the myth instead of evoking thought acts as a surrogate for it, or when, in the face of patent disintegration of the myth men spend vast amounts of time and effort in shoring it up, instead of setting out to build newer and more solid intellectual structures. The myth of the middle class has become both of these kinds of barrier to understanding. A large and uncritical group of historians complacently ascribes every major historical change in the Tudor period—and a long time before and after—to the desires, aspirations, ideas and intentions of the rising middle class; a second group turns great scholarly resources to preventing the very concept of a Tudor middle class from vaporizing before our eyes and turning into such stuff as dreams are made of.

Yet at the outset it seems more than ordinarily easy to subject the myth of the Tudors and the middle class to an empirical test. We know who the Tudors were, and what the middle class was, and we can proceed from there. Never was there a fonder illusion. The Tudors are reasonably stable but the middle class is as fluid as water. A concept that at a distance seems solid gold turns out on closer inspection to be mere melted butter.

It is only gradually that the Middle Class displays its infinite capacity for ramification. At first it appears quite innocently in association with commerce: The middle class is the "rising commercial classes," or as Professor Louis Wright puts it with commendable precision a group "whose pre-occupation was trade." Clearly we have here a bounded sector of society, sharply distinguished from the rest, a satisfactory object for discourse or investigation. We have indeed the *bourgeoisie,* precisely the group that an able 16th century Frenchman described as the *"estat moyen."* But alas as soon as we start our survey we discover that the very sponsors of the idea we wish to investigate have already obliterated most of the boundary marks, and that the middle class has begun to spread all over the social map. The two processes by which the concept is extended are a fascinating study in historical casuistry.

The first method is that of procreation, otherwise, the theory of the continuity of mercantile germ plasm. According to this theory Sir Francis Walsingham, for example, was middle class because one of his great grandfathers was a merchant, four generations on the land apparently being insufficient to attenuate the effect of merchant blood. The possibilities latent in this method of extending the middle class are enormous, and will serve to explain away dozens of otherwise anomalous facts. Does a nobleman display an aptitude for making money? We trace his pedigree through all its branches until we come on a city man, and there is our explanation. The beauty of this method is that it can be turned on and off at will. If the particular aristocrat we are investigating is a blockhead bankrupt, we can stop genealogizing short of the merchant ancestor and point to the bankruptcy as a symptom of the inevitable collapse of the old nobility before the rising middle class. The procreative theory attains its ultimate triumph perhaps when through her maternal great grandfather Geoffrey Boleyn, Lord Mayor of London, it links Queen Elizabeth herself to the middle class.

An even more useful procedure is the extension of the middle class by assimilation since it spares us an arduous and uncertain job of genealogical research. The argument, implicit rather than express, seems to run this way: The middle class were business men; business men get rich; whoever gets rich is middle class. The reasoning here might find critics among finicking logicians, but for historians on the hook between a very simple theory and some very complicated data it cannot be beat. By this reasoning the job of extending the middle class to the countryside is accomplished. Since they prospered, the copyholder of the 15th C., the leaseholder and yeoman of the 16th are drawn into the middle class, and above all the gentry, all of the gentry, even those who received titles of nobility from the Tudors. The boundaries of the middle class thus become highly elastic, and that great scholar, Professor Tawney, who did most to stretch them, takes full advantage of his own handiwork. According to the exigencies of his argument the middle class includes the copyholder or excludes him, includes the yeoman or excludes him, includes all prosperous countrymen or includes only the gentry or better. The conception of the middle class thus attains all the rigor of a rubber band. Like humpty-dumpty Professor Tawney is a master of words; middle class means what he wants it to mean.

The ultimate triumph in extending the boundaries of the middle class, however, rests with no Englishman but with Professor Louis Wright. The Tudors he has told us were a "bourgeois dynasty." Since he originally described the middle class as men of trade and the town and since the first four Tudors, uncontaminated by Boleyn blood, did not have middle class chromosomes, we note the proof of this point with interest. Henry VII he suggests was bourgeois because he had "the habits of a usurious merchant" while his son was bourgeois too because he "enjoyed his wealth with the abandon of any nouveau riche." We have here two infallible marks of the middle class—thrift and extravagance. And since in the words of the old song but in a somewhat different sense, all men are "either a little liberal or else a little conservative," we have arrived at the *ne plus ultra,* a conception of the middle class that includes the whole human race from time immemorial.

Thus has the conception of the middle class been expanded. At the risk of seeming ungrateful to my predecessors who have displayed so much ingenuity in the work, for the purpose of this paper I will try to dispense with their mighty gothic structure, in favor of a Puritan simplicity. In this paper the middle class is Seyssel's *"estat moyen,"* merchant, financier, industrialist, the town rich, the *bourgeoisie.* I am compelled to this Draconian measure by the conviction that otherwise the middle class becomes so fluid, indeed so ethereal, as to defy attempts to say anything about it.

According to the devotees of the myth of the middle class the most conspicuous evidence of the rise of that class in the Tudor period lies in the record of its land purchases. The facts alleged in support of the thesis do not admit of doubt. Tudor moralists were condemning, Tudor statesmen worrying about the extensive acquisitions of land by the merchants of their day, the extensive sales of land by its former owners. Merchants were indeed buying estates of the titled nobility and the gentry in the 16th century. On this the record clearly supports the present day historians and the contemporary moralists and statesmen. As one writer melodramatically puts it, it was a period "when an Ingram . . . could afford to buy, and a Verney was forced to sell." It is only when we consider the revolutionary implications imputed to the undeniable facts of the case that a shadow of doubt flickers through our minds. The allegations as to the facts are true; is the situation itself of earth-shaking import? Is it new?

As we approach the entrance to the Tudor era we come on our first hint that we may have misunderstood the significance of merchant land buying. William Caxton, the printer, lived most of his adult life in Flanders, where great town families spent centuries in trade. In London, he complained, there were no such mercantile dynasties. Here on the very verge of the Tudor period we find a suggestion that the exodus of business men from trade was not a peculiarity of that era. Miss Thrupp's recent study of the medieval London merchant has shown what became of the commercial families that disappeared in one, two, or three generations. Some merely died out in the male line. Some receded into obscurity, rural or urban. But a considerable number of the most considerable merchants purchased estates and set themselves up as gentlemen. Such men and their families were likely soon to be absorbed (in some instances merely reabsorbed) into the country gentry. The many

15th century London business men who died without male heirs often left behind a well-dowered widow or a few nicely fixed daughters. The Pastons, with their perpetual negotiations for London heiresses, Sir William Stonor with his two successive marriages to rich city widows, are but instances of the general truth that before the Tudor period country families had discovered the tonic effect on their more or less blue blood of a transfusion of *aurum potabile* from the city.

A century before Caxton the history of a yet more famous man of letters follows the very course which Caxton was complaining about. Father a vintner, son a vintner, public official, landlord in Kent and incidentally a poet, grandson a man of vast estates, such seems to have been the story of Geoffrey Chaucer's family. From the 14th century comes that classical example of the rise of the middle class, the de la Poles who went from trade at Hull to the Earldom of Suffolk in two generations. William de la Pole was but the brightest star in a galaxy. Lesser English financiers of Edward III's dubious ventures in conquest cap the genealogical tree of many a later aristocratic family. A refugee from the seventeenth century I lose my bearings in the strange terrain at the turn of the twelfth. Yet even in that unfamiliar region I seem to discern familiar lineaments in the misty figure of Henry Fitz Alwein, the first Lord Mayor of London. Before his Mayoralty he was a tenant in Sergentry. At his death after a long period in office, he held two knights' fees and land in four or five counties.

And so back through the centuries as far as the record will take us, we find the rising middle class making its way out to the land, buying estates from aristocrats too unlucky or thriftless to hold them. The feckless young Lord whom Chaucer's Reeve was fleecing was as utterly foredoomed to lose his land as any of his spiritual successors under Elizabeth. The gentleman waster of the 14th century poem who frittered away in an orgy of boozing and whoring estates accumulated by more prudent ancestors could have found companions in every century from the 12th to the 19th. And in the 13th century northern "Knights," including as one would expect a Percy, having their lands in hock to the Jews, found a new way to pay old debts by destroying pledge and pledgee in a common holocaust.

The process then on which historians have laid such emphasis in their account of the rise of the middle class in the Tudor period, the movement of rich merchants and industrialists out to the land, the decay of landed families and the linking of gentility with city riches by marriage, in all this there is nothing novel. Merchant Ingrams indeed were buying and landed Verneys selling at the turn of the 16th century, but our impulse to drop a tear for the passing of the old order or sing hosannah at the advent of the new is somewhat damped by the realization that only a century earlier landed Zouches and Stonors were selling, while in the person of Sir Ralph, Lord Mayor of London, merchant Verneys were buying. Indeed we are dogged by the dark suspicion that a considerable number of those ancient families declining under the Tudors were rising under Lancaster and York, the parvenus of a hundred years before, and so on, back through the centuries.

For getting and spending, gaining and losing, winning and wasting —these are not traits of one order of men or of one or two special eras of human history; they are a trait of every era when men have what other men want, of every age when some men have the strength, the cunning, and tenacity and the fortune to take what they want, while others lack the strength, the cunning, the tenacity and the fortune to keep what they have.

It remains to ask why under the circumstances historians of the Tudor era have concluded that merchant land buying in the 16th century marks an especially significant phase in the rise of the middle class. If we would understand this peculiar conclusion we would do well to recognize it not as a unique idiosyncracy but as a species of a considerable genus. One of the odder performances in contemporary historiography takes place when the social historians of *each* European century from the 12th to the 18th with an air of mystery seize the curtain cords and unveil the great secret. "Behold," they say, "in *my* century the middle class nobodies rising into the aristocracy." After an indefinite series of repetitions of this performance one is impelled to murmur, "But this is where I came in," or even, "What of it?" And then one begins to wonder why each highly competent specialist thinks that his particular sector of the apparently continuous process is so remarkable as to be worthy of the name of social revolution. Perhaps the answer is to be found in the didactic writing of contemporary moralists. Not only do Tudor writers condemn the new-made gentleman, and lament the decay of old aristocratic families; with scarcely an exception they say, or imply, that things were never thus before, that in the good old days nobles were liberal and hospitable but never prodigal; they did not sell their land. And merchants, industrious and honest, never greedy or grasping, did not seek to buy it, but were satisfied in the place to which God had called them. To historians committed to raising the middle class, willy-nilly, in the Tudor period, these denunciations of the movement as an outrageous novelty are as manna; but how much significance can we attach to them? On the face of the medieval history of land transactions, not much; on the face of the writings of earlier moralists even less.

When

> *Boys of no blood, with boast and pride,*
> *Shall wed landed ladies, and lead them at will*

Domesday is nigh, and nowadays it is clear to see "It will soon come, or perhaps is here." So sang a 14th century poet, lamenting the "novelty" of the rise of the middle class in his own age. Medieval didactic poetry of each era denounced land-getting merchants and aristocrats who married business fortunes as new things of evil, just as from age to age the process so denounced was itself continuous.

Why the moralists themselves for centuries blandly ignored the facts of the past in favor of elegant fictions we can only conjecture. Perhaps they did not ignore the facts of the past as they understood them. Their social ideal was the hierarchical society of fixed social orders, and such a society they found in the "histories" which were their regular diet—the romances of chivalry. Here was indeed the society of the moralists' dream, where knights were liberal and generous, town folk industrious and humble, peasants docile and dutiful, a society above all without an economy, where there were no scarce goods, no getting and spending, always enough for everybody in his appointed place. This cloud-cuckoo land may be a world of dream to us; to many men up through the 16th century it was no dream at all but a fact as living, more living, than anything that had actually happened in the days long before their birth. When Henry VII named his first son Arthur he was not making a casual courtesy to a lightly held fairy story; he was trying to attach his new dynasty to that segment of the past which contemporary Englishmen most vividly knew. Like Mark Twain, medieval men remembered best the things that had not happened.

When we have proceeded so far in our analysis of the myth of the middle class, we run head on into the indisputable fact of drastic agrarian change in the 16th century—the so-called agrarian revolution. The commercialization and rationalization of agriculture, the decline of subsistence farming, the new literature on farm improvement, crop specialization, scientific surveying, enclosure, rackrenting, sheep-farming, the decay of hospitality, the replacement of the intimate, the personal, the customary, the medieval relationship between lord and man by the cold cash nexus of employer and laborer or hireling farmer (the typical economic form of middle class capitalism)—these are the symptoms of change. The whole process is shot through with the appetite for gain and the cold, rational pursuit of profit, alien to the sleepy, custom-bound countryside, native to the bustle and business habits of the city. The agricultural revolution is simply what happens when the rising middle class of the town turns its attention to the exploitation of land for profit. And thus to the support of the legend of the rocketing middle class and the plummeting aristocracy comes the fable of the city slicker and the rube, the clever, ruthless Londoner and the pudding-headed country-man. The combination is a most happy bit of economy in scholarship, since precisely the same evidence used in defense of the legend—the financial embarrassments of aristocrats, the land purchases of mer-chants—can be trotted out and used again to defend the fable.

Of course if one looks for indebted peers and bankrupt knights in the Tudor period one finds them; but then in the records of the debtors' court all classes are always equally bankrupt. If instead of looking for the economic lame ducks of the landed aristocracy in the places where we are sure to find them, we move in a less constricted circle our incom-petents are offset by men of a different stamp, men who export cloth, invest in the metallurgical industry and coal mining, improve the tin smelting process, work at fen draining and save 10,000 acres of bottom land by a new cut in the Bridgewater River. On the shady fringes of legality no doubt but in the bright sunlight of profit we find aristocratic corn broggers, enclosers, and rackrenters. Among these enterprising rubes are many old families and but few parvenus in the ordinary sense. But historians of the rise of the middle class use the terms "parvenu" and "old aristocracy" in a sense different from that of ordinary discourse —in a Pickwickian sense indeed. In common speech a parvenu is a man of recent riches or gentility; and the title of old aristocrat is reserved for men with long pedigrees. But for those who write of the rise of the middle class a gentleman who is not a blithering incompetent about his own affairs becomes thereby a parvenu though his acres were in his family since the conquest. Conversely, he who is sufficiently a fool to lose the lands his father won becomes an old aristocrat by his virtuosity in stupidity, though the paint is barely dry on his blazon.

An early 16th century letter from a landlord to his steward typifies that commercial spirit which city men are supposed to have brought with them to the land. Amid a mass of other minutiae the steward is instructed to sell off a £100 of timber out of a wood in Amersham, reserving the best to the owner. He is to get "Thomas Bynks the carpenter of London" to go to Amersham with him "to help drive the most to our profit." He is also to try to arrange with Lord Brooks an exchange of one of his employer's estates for the lordship of Wardere. And he is to attach Sir John Pickering's goods and arrest him for debt. And so on with infinite particulars. This painstaking attention to detail, this thorough knowledge of the state of his own affairs, this appetite for the last possible farthing of profit, this ruthless treatment of an unfortunate debt-ridden gentleman, do they not all bespeak the merchant, stirring the stagnant, medieval countryside with the spirit of capitalist exploitation? In theory, perhaps, but in fact the man who wrote the letter was Edward Stafford, 3rd Duke of Buckingham, premier Duke and one of the most active enclosers and depopulators in all England.

We need not be surprised. Hard-headed, tight-fisted landlordism was not an innovation of the Tudor merchant or for that matter of the Tudor age. When we cross the threshold of the middle ages the latent signs of vigorous economic initiative on the land are unmistakably marked in action, although the thought and spirit that lay behind the act can only be inferred. Too easily we conceive of the changes in medieval rural life as large impersonal secular movements. We forget that underlying those changes were a multitude of individual decisions on the wisdom of which depended in some measure the future course of events and entirely the success or failure of the men who did the deciding. Did a small 12th century landlord try to stand on his rights to labor service in the face of a tight labor market? He lost his labor force. If he was unduly obstinate he lost his land soon, too, since idle acres then as now make bankrupt landlords. The loss of incompetents is the gain of the economic opportunists among the landed whose enterprises for clearing, ditching, and draining their land helped to make the 12th century and 13th century agrarian history the tale of a vast land reclamation project. By the same token the lord who failed to take advantage of the labor glut of the 13th century to shift his relations with the peasantry in the light of the altered situation lost ground before others more acute or more ruthless than he. The hundred-year long depression that lasted past the middle of the 15th century with its shrinking markets and depopulation meant dark days for landlords who did not trim their sails to the economic hurricane. And the halcyon times of the Tudors demanded a new economic strategy of the landowner, if he was to survive—loosening the rigid economic structure that as a matter of self-preservation his predecessors had imposed on his estates. The very phrase "agricultural revolution" while it casts doubt on the landlord's scrupulosity abundantly testifies to his vigor and adaptability. To all the vicissitudes of four eventful centuries then the landlords had to accommodate themselves, or, as many did with each secular economic swing, lose their lands to men with a better head for managing their affairs.

For through all the changes in late medieval economy and social organization land was bought, sold and exchanged in a market at least as free as that of the town. And no device has yet been found superior to a free market for squeezing out along with the unfortunate, those who are incompetent, lazy and unresourceful while rewarding the lucky, the busy and the enterprising.

The qualities that enabled a few families to hold their own on the land through the centuries are distinctly marked in the estate book of Henry de Bray about 1300. There we can watch in action the preservation and improvement of an estate, that, passing to the Dives family through Henry's daughter was to remain there to the Civil War. Henry was a 500-acre man. His rent roll did not raise him to the level of a knight. Two or three centuries later he would have called himself esquire. He was proto-gentry. And he showed that proclivity for accumulation and for driving hard bargains that was to cause harassed peasants centuries later to feel there would never be good times while gentlemen were up. He went into the land-market in his neighborhood when he was a young man, and stayed in it for thirty years. He sold, exchanged, and bought, but in about 30 transactions his purchases were four times the number of his sales. By successive payments in three years he cut the rents on one of his large holdings by eleven twelfths. For a period of twenty years Henry put an average of one third of his rental income into building. Scarcely more than a fifth of his outlay for construction went to making himself a house. Most of the rest went into farm building—granges, pig sties, walls, water-courses, bridges, granaries, tenants' cottages. His mill brought him 10% a year on his investment, a fact carefully noted in his estate book. Henry moreover had picked up enough law to serve as steward for a Northampton priory.

Henry de Bray did not need urban background to make him an enterprising gentleman farmer with a business-like appetite for methodical gain. In the 15th century Sir William Stonor, heir to several generations of Cotswold graziers, long substantial men in their neighborhood, showed an even more vivid flair for entrepreneurship. By judicious marriages and business arrangements he set himself at the head of a vertically organized wool business. The clip of Sir William Stonor's Cotswold flock was sold at Calais by the firm of Sir William Stonor and associates, Merchants of the Staple. But before he became a merchant and after he ceased to be one Sir William was an improving landowner, whose permanent concern was estate management. His goal was to become "the worshipfullest of the Stonors" that ever was. Two city marriages and a plunge into the wool trade were no bar to his aspiration. He crowned his career and achieved his goal by a third marriage to Anne Neville, niece of the Earl of Warwick, the King Maker.

Need we believe then that the 16th century equivalents of Bray and Stonor had to wait on urban merchant inspiration before they embarked on the course that created an economic upheaval in the English countryside? Certainly some of the older aristocracy did not wait on much nudging from the townsmen to take advantage of the opportunity that the expansion of the woolen industry offered the landlords. In the government's earliest investigation of depopulation it found Brook, Lord Cobham, Grey, Marquess of Dorset, and Sacheveralls, Belknaps, and Hampdens among the active enclosers. And in truth the basic procedures that wrought the agricultural revolution of the 16th century were not veiled mysteries of commerce accessible only to merchants. To throw up a hedge and throw out a tenant; to run sheep into a field, to hoist rents and raise entry fines: these were not strokes requiring economic genius or merchant lore or even moderate intelligence. The stupidest and the most extravagant lout of a landlord could do these things—as the stupidest and most extravagant often did.

"I showed myself to my friends in court and after went down to my tenants and surveyed my lands, let new leases, took their money, spent it" in London "upon ladies, and now I can take up at my pleasure." So speaks a character in *Epicœne*. Ben Jonson had a name for him. It was Sir Amorous LaFoole.

We have had under observation two related processes of English social history throughout several centuries: first the acquisition of land by merchants, middle class industrialists and financiers, second the loss of land by those whose families had held extensive properties long enough to be considered and consider themselves members of the landed aristocracy. That sector of the movement which falls within the Tudor period manifests no peculiarities that warrant setting it off from the general process; but the process over its whole course is one of the most important phenomena in English social history.

For centuries it adversely affected the middle class in the three main ways a group can be affected—in personnel, materiel and morale. As to personnel some of the most competent members of the middle class were constantly being skimmed off and thereby the complex web of established commercial connections and know-how was continuously being snapped. On the level of materiel—the economic level—we have the story centuries long of the drain of capital from commerce and industry to land. Extensive capital accumulations won in the town were spilled out onto the countryside instead of going to finance commercial and industrial expansion. What may be involved is not merely a run of cash from city to country, but a continuous constriction of credit as the men whose success had raised their credit high moved slowly but steadily out of trade.

The effect of access to gentility through land acquisition on middle class morale was ambivalent. In one direction it ran a floor under that morale. The preachers in the pulpit might thunder against mercantile greed, the Church look with a somewhat jaundiced eye on all the processes by which a business man got rich, yet to men not blind to the glories of this world, the transactions that opened the way to them could scarcely appear contemptible, let beggarly friars say what they would.

But as a concomitant to the floor under middle class morale went a ceiling over it. By moving out to the land the merchant might soon become a gentleman; by the same token, however, he soon ceased to be one of the middle class. When a merchant bought a large estate he was, and he knew it, buying his way out of his class. Such course of action is destructive of a sense of class solidarity. It is hard to feel unlimited pride in a group whose leading members are fleeing it so persistently. The direction of the flight of the successful men—to the land directly or indirectly—left those who stayed behind no possible doubt as to where they stood. It was a social signpost unmistakably pointing out to the land: This Way Up. Far then from testifying to the growth in power of the middle class the process we have examined involved a triple operation upon it—decapitation, exsanguination and removal of the backbone. Differing from human beings, social groups survive such surgery but only on a relatively feeble, pallid, invertebrate level.

The open door to gentility then was a sort of escape hatch whereby the middle class was kept to size. The steady traffic on the social ladder was not a sign that the ladder was shaky or that the rungs had come unstuck; it was on the contrary one of the surest signs that the ladder was stable and the rungs tight.

The place where the actual relations between social groups most effectively display themselves is perhaps at the point of tension or friction between them. Then attitudes buried under layers of amenities in times of harmony are uncovered and displayed. Consequently the letter of an aggrieved knight to the merchant rulers of a borough throws more light than volumes of routine correspondence on the attitude of the rural aristocracy to the urban middle class. Such a letter Sir George Grey wrote in the 1590's to the rulers of Leicester about a felon they had taken into custody contrary to what Sir George regarded as their right. "Have him I will," he wrote the mayor ". . . therefore send him me, for as I live I will try all the friends I have in England, but I will be righted of this your fond and unjust dealing with me . . . you and your brethren have already annoyed me and all the rest of Her Majesty's justices in the shire in taking out of my hands what neither belonged to you nor your shallow capacities could understand . . . You and your town have no reason to offer me this wrong . . . for if you be able to cross me in one thing I can requite your town with twenty, and therefore I wish you not to begin with me, for as I am a gentleman I will be revenged one way or another to my contentment and to your dislikes." To the consternation of the merchant oligarchy, Sir George was as good as his word. He got himself appointed to the commission for assessing the town's subsidy, and all their efforts to dislodge him from the post were in vain. His riposte to the town of Leicester was more than brutal rhetoric. When he said, "If you be able to cross me in one thing, I can requite you in twenty," he was performing a rough but an accurate piece of social analysis.

The elder Cecil once received a nervous and apologetic letter from the Lord Mayor of London that reveals the obverse of the Leicester affair. The mayor understands that Her Majesty and the nobles have taken offense at the "excessive spending of venison and other victuals" in the Halls of the Livery Companies. Therefore Common Council has now forbidden excessive feasts and the consumption of venison in the Halls. The major leak of venison, however, is into the taverns, "resorts of the meaner sort." The mayor has drawn up an act to cover the taverns too, "If your lordship have liking thereof." The psychology of the Tudor middle class could scarcely be more sharply revealed. There is no law or command from above involved here, only an expression of annoyance at the presumption of the Livery Companies in showing a taste for display that is the prerogative of the aristocracy. On the other side there is no protest, no claim of right or complaint of its infringe-

ment. Only the immediate, docile compliance of the habitual subordinate, and the habitual subordinate's usual trick of laying the blame on
his inferiors—"the meaner sort." These pliable, humble men, who are
they? The members of the Livery Companies, the Common Council,
the Lord Mayor of London himself—altogether the *crème de la crème*
of the Tudor *bourgeoisie*. And here indeed we have their spiritual
measure. One only has to remember how the middle class in the 19th
century, hungry for game, made a shambles of the two hundred year
old game laws, over the vain protest of the aristocracy. In Elizabeth's
day that bullet did not have enough of the powder of middle class
morale behind it to discommode a chipmunk.

There is little evidence then that the Tudor period saw any extraor-
dinary development in the middle class of group consciousness, group
pride, or will to power. Of princely concern for the welfare of the
middle class and favor to its members the evidence is abundant. Tudor
sovereigns elevated merchants and sons of merchants to positions of high
public trust; they took a myriad of measures to foster commerce and
industry, they granted extensive privileges to certain merchant groups;
and finally, they more than once asserted that the welfare of the commonwealth stood in trade.

By concentrating on this set of particulars a historian can make a
strong case for the theory that the Tudors especially favored the middle
class. But it is not the historian's business to draw from one set of particulars conclusions that an equally available second set will modify or
cancel. Tudor statesmen of middle class origin completely dissociated
themselves and their interests from those of the middle class; Tudor
princes put embargoes on the export business as expedients of diplomatic pressure and held the Flanders fleet to ransom to impose fiscal
obligations on the English cloth merchants. The privileges they granted
to one set of merchants were usually at the expense of another set of
merchants or an equally middle class group of petty industrial entrepreneurs. And if on occasion they referred to the merchants as the chief
pillars of the commonwealth, this was an accolade they tended to bestow
rather liberally on various groups from yeomen to sailors as the momentary exigencies of rhetoric required. The same momentary exigencies
occasionally transformed the mercantile pillars of the commonwealth
into cormorants and greedy, grasping gripers in royal pronunciamentos.

Despite apparent antithesis in word and action, the Tudor attitude
toward the middle class was neither self-contradictory nor ambiguous,
but intelligible and consistent in the light of Tudor policy. Although

occasionally distorted by the immediate imperatives of war, diplomacy and defense, perverted by fiscal stringencies and inhibited by a tough legal structure of which the Henrys and Elizabeth were remarkably respectful, Tudor policy was fundamentally coherent and solid. Well it might be, since it was erected on old and deep-set ideas. The hierarchical organic conception of society, once the scholastic idealization of 13th century realities, then in the waning middle ages the vehicle of a vigorous social criticism, becomes with the Tudors the mold of policy, the guide to action. To implement a social ideal older than Thomas Aquinas they brought a faith in the efficacy of governmental regulation as naive as our own. The world was out of joint, and men being sinful creatures, it would always tend to get out of joint, but the Tudors had no doubt that they were born to set it right. What was new about Tudor policy lay not in the social theory at its base, but in its magnification of the active regulatory work of the prince as the means by which society might approximate its own ideal. That ideal was organic: society was comprised of members performing different functions for the common good. The ideal was also hierarchical: though all parts of the commonwealth were indispensable they were not equal, but differed in degree and excellence as well as in kind. The role of policy was to maintain and support good order as good order had been understood for several centuries—social peace and harmony in a status-based society.

To this end royal policy was to advance the prosperity of all estates and remedy their legitimate grievances. On the negative side it was relentlessly to repress violent breaches of order, riot, sedition, and rebellion, and to subject unregulated desires and particular interests of individuals and groups to the good order and harmony of the commonwealth. Apparent inconsistencies in Tudor policy are merely expressions of its positive and negative sides. The Tudors did not believe that the governing power should align itself on the side of one class and against another. From the point of view of Tudor social theory such an assumption is wicked and perverse. Seditions and trouble, the bane of commonwealths, are not prevented but encouraged by such alliances. They drive the oppressed to rebellion out of desperation and encourage the oppressor to sedition out of arrogance. The conspiracies of the overmighty and the wild violence of the base are but heads and tails of the same coin—a disordered commonwealth.

Tudor policy usually was quite tender of vested interest. It protected old ones and created new ones in the emergent forms of enterprise. It thus established itself in a regulatory position *vis-à-vis* the whole range of commercial and industrial life. Vested interests should be protected and the more vested the more protected, since to such interests the hopes, aspirations, and security of so many men were bound. The idea that a whole local industry should be wiped out because the same goods could be produced cheaper elsewhere made no sense to the Tudors, and if their economics was rather crude, their knowledge of the cost of suppressing the riots and rebellions of men thrown out of work, being founded in experience, was most precise. A well-regulated trade and a well-regulated industry were simply corollaries of a well-regulated commonwealth, just as a well-regulated agriculture was. It was not Tudor policy either to stand mulishly athwart the path of change, or to allow it free rein, but to guide it, to bring it as they said to some good rule comfortable with good order. The vast mass of Tudor legislation on economic activities rests solidly on three principles—privilege, regulation, supervision. The purpose was to prevent the unchecked greed and ambition of any group—middle class or other—from dislocating the social order.

The men of the middle class had an important function in this organic hierarchical commonwealth, as the leading people of the towns, "the better sort," the abler people. The Tudors were glad to see the governments of municipalities in their hands. They encouraged that drift toward merchant oligarchy which antedated the accession of Henry VII. The closed corporation put the merchant above the craftsman in governance, as he should be. It well comported with Tudor conceptions to concentrate the administration of the towns in the hands of the richer few, it did not comport with such conceptions for the central government to repose blind faith in its chosen instruments. If according to Tudor theory it was a part of good policy to rely on "the better sort" in ruling the towns, it was equally a part of good policy to suspect that the better sort would abuse the trust reposed in them, that they would become overbearing and tyrannical, acting in their own interest against that of the lesser folk. The Privy Council did not deal gently with middle class oligarchs whose misconduct of local affairs was a grievance to the poor. Nor did it gladly suffer town councils that could not rule without faction and disorder whatever the cause. Such councils were likely to find themselves under chilly scrutiny by a few of the neighboring gentry bearing a special commission from the Crown to look into the situation with a view to bringing it to order. Therein the Tudors indicated both the tentative character of their reliance on the middle class and the place they reserved for it in the social order.

In the good policy of the well-ordered commonwealth the middle class had a further role assigned to it. As a contemporary observer noted, the government had "policies to enrich the merchant and artizan by statute and law made for their benefits for which they give the prince a great sum of money and yearly rent and also get them great wealth thereby to be more able to contribute to the subsidies, taxes and wars."

To transfer the organic analogy to the barnyard, the Tudors regarded the middle class as the milch herd of the commonwealth. They had firmly grasped the sound lactogenic principle propagated by a present day dairy that contented cows give more milk. They carefully tended their herd as long as it docilely did what was required of it, but woe to the milker that forgot its place and imagined that the attention it received licensed it to act like a bull in a china shop. We may close our investigation of the attitude of the Tudors toward the middle class with a tragi-comic illustration—the story of Henry VIII and the recalcitrant Londoner.

In 1544 with his finances groaning under the strain of war Henry had asked for a benevolence for the prosecution of the campaign against Scotland. In the whole Court of Aldermen one man alone, Richard Reed, had the gumption or presumption to refuse to be benevolent despite all persuasion and reasoning. A milch cow was refusing to be milked, a habit Henry was loath to encourage. He had no taste for a merchant who "for the defense of the realm and for the continuance of his quiet life . . . could not find in his heart to disburse a small quantity of his substance." He felt that Richard Reed had better do "some service for his country with his body whereby he might be somewhat instructed of the difference between sitting quietly in his house and the travail and danger which others do daily sustain." So in the middle of January he dispatched the Alderman "unto School" to the Warden of the Middle Marches, "there to serve as a soldier . . . at his own charge" in the Scottish campaign. With fine pedagogic zeal Henry added that to ensure Reed's education the Warden was to put him into positions of "ordinary dangers and in such a place in garrison as he may feel what pains other poor soldiers abide abroad in the King's service." The lesson seems to have been faithfully administered, since the next we hear of Alderman Reed he is a prisoner of war of the enemy. This unplanned extension course probably gave the unlucky Alderman during the long Northern winter ample opportunity well to understand in what sense and for what purposes the Tudors relied on the middle class.

With the misadventures of the Alderman Reed, the sturdy bourgeois born three hundred years too soon, we may close our investigation of the myth of the middle class in Tudor England. In all I have said there has been no intention to deny the historical importance of the rise of the middle class. In the war of words preceding the reform bill of 1832, one proponent after another of that measure argued that its peculiar merit lay in placing the borough franchise in the hands of those pre-eminently fit by their character and virtues to control the political destinies of England. The provisions for borough franchise in that bill did in effect transfer the right to choose a majority in the House of Commons to the group whose right to the designation of middle class I will not deny. Here indeed the spokesmen for the middle class demanded for it a sort of hegemony over English society. But Henry VIII had been mouldering in his grave for nearly three centuries, Elizabeth for two and a half. In the 19th century an assertive, self-confident, politically alert, over-whelmingly rich social class was demanding its place in the sun of power and prestige. In the 16th century the most successful members of an amorphous congeries of non-agrarian economic groups, all modest in mien and modest in pretensions, were clambering out of their groups into the place where the sun was, and long was to remain, among the landed gentlemen and noblemen of England. It is not the purpose of this paper to explain the phenomena of 1832, but only to say of Tudor England, it was not then, it was not there.

It could hardly be then or there as long as the middle class gave unwavering credit to a hierarchical organic conception of society, which irresistibly placed the ultimate goal of middle class striving not within the class but beyond it.

BIBLIOGRAPHY

Bernard Bailyn, *The New England Merchants in the Seventeenth Century*, Cambridge, Mass, 1955.

Sidney A. Burrell, "Calvinism, Capitalism, and the Middle Classes: Some Afterthoughts on an Old Problem," *The Journal of Modern History*, XXXII (1960), 129–141.

J. H. Hexter, "The Myth of the Middle Class in Tudor England," in Hexter, *Reappraisals in History*, Evanston, 1961. [This is the much expanded version of the essay printed here.]

——, "Storm Over the Gentry," in Hexter, *Reappraisals in History*, Evanston, 1961.

R. H. Tawney, "The Rise of the Gentry, 1558–1640," *Economic History Review*, XI (1941), 1–38.

Sylvia L. Thrupp, *The Merchant Class of Medieval London,* Chicago, 1948.

H. R. Trevor-Roper, "The Gentry, 1540–1640," *Economic History Review,* Supplement 1, 1953.

THE COMPOSITION OF THE NEW BUREAUCRATIC ELITE IN PRUSSIA *

Hans Rosenberg

During at least the last five or six centuries, the tasks required for the running of the centralized and competent modern state have required men of talent. When the established families of the upper classes have not been able to supply able men for these governmental positions, the positions have fallen open to men of talent from lower social classes. Social mobility through government service has, therefore, been a constant source of social rising in European history for a long time. Rosenberg illustrates these typical processes very well with his account of the rise and staffing of the modern Prussian state.

Hans Rosenberg, who has taught at Brooklyn College, is now Professor of History at the University of California at Berkeley. He specializes in the political and economic aspects of German and Central European history.

With the formation of large administrative and military bureaucracies, a delicate and unstable balance was struck in government employment between commoners and the heirs of superior social rank. It was generally characteristic of the rising absolute monarchies that a considerable percentage of the "new bureaucrats" was supplied by "illborn" persons and, except for France, also by foreign, in preference to native, nobles. Men of such defective background were more dependent upon, and therefore more obedient to, the royal authority.

* Reprinted by permission of the publishers, from Hans Rosenberg, *Bureaucracy, Aristocracy and Autocracy: The Prussian Experience, 1680–1815,* Cambridge: Harvard University Press, Copyright 1958 by the President and Fellows of Harvard College.

The diverse composition of the executive elite of the Hohenzollerns reflected, in accord with this continental trend, the bewildering currents of social mobility. However, the gathering of a "Prussian" staff of professional administrators under monarchical control did not involve a sudden or radical break with the past when almost only men with long pedigrees had access to the spoils of "public service." A more flexible policy had gained ground in parochial Brandenburg during the first half of the seventeenth century. Almost all the members of the elector's privy council, founded in 1604 to circumvent the influence of Junkerdom, were either foreign noblemen or commoners. Yet it was here that the ancient *status quo* was restored on the eve of the transition to monarchical absolutism by reserving the majority of all significant government positions for native nobles. The reorganization of the privy council, in 1651, was preceded by a social purge. In 1640, the ratio of nonnobles to nobles in the council had been five to three. A decade later it was only one to five. Of the thirty-four privy councilors appointed from 1653 until 1687, only seven were commoners.[1] Some of the latter, moreover, felt themselves suppressed and stigmatized by their ancestor-conscious colleagues. The relative position of the lowborn in the upper ranks of the General War Commissariat was stronger, if not only the War Commissars proper, but also the *commissarii loci,* the predecessors of the *Steuerräte,* are included in the reckoning.[2] But on the whole, the founder of Prussian absolutism, because of social prejudice, personal preference, and political expediency, set aside the most distinguished civil state employments for nobles of old lineage, mostly Junkers.

Even accurate statistics can be quite deceptive. The numerical preponderance of the "blood nobility" in the councils of Elector Frederick William obscures the fact that after 1660, during the absolutist phase of his career, bureaucrats of middle class origin were his chief political advisers and diplomatic assistants. In the 1640's, a Brandenburgian Junker soldier, von Burgsdorff, had guided his young prince. In the 1650's, Count Waldeck and, then, a Pomeranian nobleman, Otto von Schwerin, served virtually as a one-man "brain trust." But after 1660 the tide turned against the increasingly anachronistic survivors of the old *Ständestaat* regime. During the 1660's, a former university professor,

---

[1] G. Oestreich, *Der brandenburg-preussische Geheime Rat,* 29–30; F. L. Carsten, *Origins of Prussia,* 178, 180, 182, 257–58.

[2] For the details see F. Wolters, *Brandenburgischen Finanzen,* II, 106ff., 112ff., 145ff., 159ff.

Friedrich Jena, was the "suggesting" deputy prime minister. When his star declined, he gave way to another commoner, Franz Meinders, who held his own for about fifteen years, until he was overshadowed by still another scheming ex-professor, Paul Fuchs.

The numerical balance between the high and lowborn in the civil bureaucracy was reversed in the course of the first half of the eighteenth century. The political entrepreneurship of Frederick William I turned out to be a golden age for select men of common origin. He created chances for advancement unmatched in Prussian government employment until the 1920's when the Prussian state was a stronghold of the Social Democrats. To increase his personal power and to speed up the subjugation of the old official hierarchy; to demonstrate to the titled aristocracy that there were limits to its indispensability; to prevent a sagging of ambitions in the service of the crown, he gave qualified priority to pliable nonnobles in the civil establishments.

Thus, in filling the functionally important positions in the administrative bureaucracy, he largely relied on men who could not boast of ancestors who, even before the Hohenzollerns had settled down in eastern Germany, had been masters of the land. Frederick William I was bent on preventing monarchical absolutism from being a mockery. Like Frederick III of Denmark, Charles XI of Sweden, Louis XIV of France, and Peter of Russia, he was drawn to men whom he could make and unmake and, therefore, use effectively as tools in the pursuit of a policy of domesticating the native nobility. Hence the "common intruders" were called upon to keep a watchful eye on the predatory *seigneurs*, the Junker *officiers* and the squire judges in the higher courts who, in the past, had banded together in converting a large part of the dynastic patrimony into a wonderful means of making a cavalier-like living. All this, combined with the drive for the raising of professional quality, accounts for the sharply marked ascendancy of social parvenus in the civil state service from 1713 to 1740.

All the private secretaries and personal assistants of Frederick William I, holding the rank of secretary or councilor in his "cabinet" (*Kabinettssekretär* or *Kabinettsrat*), were commoners.[3] Even Frederick II, who otherwise yielded to the resurgence of the nobility in government, did not touch this job monopoly set apart for men of low birth. Although he broke away from the practice of his predecessor to make ministers (Creutz, Thulemeier, Marschall, Boten) out of cabinet

---

[3] Hermann Hüffer, "Die Beamten des älteren preussischen Kabinetts von 1713–1808," *Forschungen*, V (1892), 157–190.

officers, he did not allow a nobleman to become a cabinet councilor, that is, to be a clerk, one able to pull wires behind the curtain in the king's personal office, the cabinet.

Of the one hundred and eighteen functionaries outside Berlin listed in 1737 as councilors and directors of the various Boards of War and Domains, only thirty-six were noble.[4] No other Prussian government until the destruction of the monarchy had at the summit of the executive hierarchy a larger percentage of social *nouveaux arrivés* than Frederick William's General Directory, foreign office, and department of justice and church affairs, the three collegiate agencies which had come to constitute the chief divisions of the reorganized central administration.[5]

In 1723, in the newly founded General Directory, the nine noble privy councilors, whose function and official rank corresponded to that of the *maîtres des requêtes* in France, still held the margin over their eight nonnoble colleagues. Conversely, by 1740, of eighteen privy councilors only three were wellborn. And as for the ministers themselves, the men with common parents rose as a group to a relative position which put them slightly above parity with those of their professional peers who came from old noble families. The numerical superiority of the lowborn in the upper ranks of the administrative bureaucracy of King Frederick William did not make them the politically most effective group in the monocratically directed state, let alone in the Prussian community. Reversely, their numerical insignificance in the days of the Elector Frederick William had been disproportionate to the strong political role which men of their kind had played after 1660. Thus, the nobility of descent had lost ground, in terms of influence and numbers, in the exercise of the powers of leadership.

But in several crucial corners of the professionalized state service the First Estate reasserted under Frederick William I its time-honored claim to preëminence and privileged treatment in public life. Of the presidencies of the new Boards of War and Domains all but one were held by noblemen of old lineage. Within the framework of the absolute monarchy's provincial administration, therefore, the richest rewards and the highest responsibilities were from the beginning a noble preserve. In order to facilitate, on the provincial level, the enforcement of royal policy, it proved indeed opportune to appoint as top officials old-

---

[4] *Forschungen*, XLIX (1937), 233–234.
[5] For a complete list of the Prussian ministers from 1848 to 1918, see *Handbuch über den preussischen Staat*, CXXXVI (Berlin, 1930), 99–104.

established Junkers, especially if they had been reoriented in the Royal Prussian Army prior to their transfer to the civil bureaucracy.

These board presidents were not merely key administrators who happened to own landed estates. They were also "commissioned professional politicians," who had a political function which was as important as it was difficult. It was their job to end antagonism and conflict in the rural districts by securing the loyal support of the squire-*Landräte*, who linked the central administration to the mighty village masters who had to be won over to the royal cause. Within their private law dominion these local autocrats continued to unite in a single focus of power landownership, proprietary public authority, and high social position. Thus, the presidents were strategically placed liaison officers in aristocratic public relations. They were intimately associated with the cardinal task of cementing the interpenetration of the new political system of centralized despotism and of the old order of Junker home rule. Consequently, the board presidents were, throughout the eighteenth century, often the equals and sometimes even the superiors of the ministers in Berlin in prestige, influence, and official recognition.

More clearcut than the uneven distribution of administrative "commissions" among the high and lowborn was the trend of personnel replenishment in the military service class. Under the resolute leadership of Frederick William I, the heterogeneous body of mercenary army officers was converted into a closely knit corps of aristocrats. Formerly the opportunities accorded to "talent" or, in other words, to "illborn" *officiers de fortune* had been broad enough to bring to the dinner table of the Elector Frederick William three peasant sons, the generals Derfflinger, Hennigs, and Lüdcke. The avenues were now closed by the same Frederick William I who opened the gates of the civil state to careerists of humble social origin. He restricted or eliminated altogether the "undesirables" in the armed forces, that is, in the tactful language of Frederick II, the "nonnoble riff-raff." In consequence, the nobility gradually attained almost a complete monopoly over all commissions from the rank of captain upwards.[6] This was

---

[6] See Max Lehmann, *Scharnhorst*, II (Leipzig, 1887), 56–57, 644; Reinhold Koser, *König Friedrich der Grosse*, I (Stuttgart, 1893), 531ff.; II, 2 (1903), 505–6; Curt Jany, *Geschichte der Königlich Preussischen Armee bis zum Jahre 1807*, I (Berlin, 1928), 722–725; Max Jähns, *Geschichte der Kriegswissenschaften*, II (Munich, 1890), 1635–36. By 1804, there were only two nonnobles among the 422 staff and general officers of the infantry. Of the corresponding 276 cavalry officers, only four hussars were without noble rank. Calculated on the basis of *Kurzgefasste Stamm- und Rangliste der Kgl. Preussischen Armee 1804* (Berlin, 1805).

political capital profitably invested: it lured the hitherto decisive social force in the community, the independent Junker class, into the dynastic-bureaucratic state where, as Frederick II put it, *"la guerre est un métier de gens d'honneur."* [7]

The composition of the civil and military service elites of the Hohenzollern state was indicative of some of the major social changes which crystallized everywhere with the growth of the monarch's personal powers and of bureaucratic organization on a large scale. Since absolute government and the expansion of the dynastic labor market opened up fresh sources of differentiation, the stratification of society grew more complex. By giving rise to novel segments of the governing class, absolutism disturbed and confused the old social system, built on birth and privilege, on hierarchy and hereditary estate distinctions (*ständische Gesellschaft*).

The new civil and military bureaucracies constituted professional classes of great functional and political importance. Hence they were recognized by their creator, the sovereign ruler, as superior status groups. Having like organizational status and a common way of life as "royal servants," they formed two distinct occupational estates (*Berufsstände*), an estate of administrative government officials (*Beamtenstand*) and an estate of military officers (*Offiziersstand*). These hierarchies of appointed and removable dynastic employees did not fit into the neatly defined divisions of the traditional society of northeastern Germany, the essential features of which had been the rigorous partition into hereditary estates (*Geburtsstände*), into closed, caste-like legal classes. In such a society "man was not man"; he was either superior, common, or inferior.

The nobility, being superior to all other groups in power, privilege, and prestige, had formed the First Estate (*Adelsstand*), the upper class. The commoners or burghers, i.e., the permanent town residents subject to municipal law and administration, being only "second class people" in influence and rights, had constituted the Second Estate (*Bürgerstand*), the middle class, inferior to the nobility but superior to the peasantry. At the bottom of the scale had stood the "inferiors," the Third Estate (*Bauernstand*), identical with the rural masses, mostly peasant serfs.[8]

---

[7] *Oeuvres de Frédéric le Grand,* IX (Berlin, 1848), 106.

[8] These social status divisions continued to prevail until 1807 when they were largely liquidated by the famous October Edict. As for the numerical strength of

The formation of new upper class strata, made up of the holders of the higher positions in the civil and military bureaucracies, complicated social rankings. But their emergence also reacted on the relations between social stratification and political hierarchy. By their very existence and by virtue of the heterogeneous social antecedants of their personnel, the service estates challenged the complacent illusion that inherited superior status and ownership of a landed estate as such assured the right to rule as well as fitness for leadership and managerial ability.

Even titled aristocrats were now impelled, before they were entrusted with definite duties, to give the impression of competence. This requirement often aroused hurt feelings in the circles of the large landed proprietors, infuriated by any violation of noble privileges, especially where "places" and the "right of the native-born" were at stake.[9]

The competitive struggle for professional advancement and individual social success among the bureaucratic partisans of absolute government gave birth to a type of functionary more opportunistic and more "rational" than the *Ständestaat officier* had been. Within the royal service careful calculation of personal chances and the adoption of rules of behavior designed to outwit and trip up rivals by shrewdness, superior performance, intrigue, or eel-like maneuvering, came to be typical ingredients of "personal ability," "special skills," and "efficiency."[10] For the persevering climber it was not enough to learn self-discipline. He had to make a methodical attempt to appraise his professional colleagues and superiors in terms of their fluctuating "value" and the influence of their relatives, friends, and cliques. In short, he had to be a special kind of social and political arithmetician.

---

the hereditary estates and the occupational estates on the eve of the Stein-Hardenberg reforms, see Leopold Krug, *Abriss der neuesten Statistik des preussischen Staats* (Halle, 1804), 18.

[9] For a typical illustration, see *Urkunden und Aktenstücke zur Geschichte des Kurfürsten Friedrich Wilhelm,* XVI (1899), 1004ff., 1014.

[10] For descriptive detail, see M. Philippson, *Der Grosse Kurfürst Friedrich Wilhelm von Brandenburg,* III (Berlin, 1903), 14–15, 40–55; C. Hinrichs, *Friedrich Wilhelm I,* 111ff.; Theodor Fontane, *Wanderungen durch die Mark Brandenburg,* II (Berlin, 1868), 90ff. A penetrating generalized comment on this process of readjusting the modes of social behavior to the trend of political centralization under dynastic leadership, in Norbert Elias, *Ueber den Prozess der Zivilisation,* II (Basel, 1939), 370ff. See also Max Handman, "The Bureaucratic Culture Pattern and Political Revolution," *The American Journal of Sociology,* XXXIX (1933), 301–313; Alexander Rüstow, *Ortsbestimmung der Gegenwart. Eine universalgeschichtliche Kulturkritik,* I (Erlenbach-Zürich, 1950), 241–246.

He could not get ahead without the favor of prominent influence peddlers in the good graces of the absolute prince, the chief dispenser of power, emoluments, social prestige, and other favors.

The "new bureaucrat," as a social type, was well represented by the aides of Frederick William, the Elector, and of his immediate successor. These restless, intensely selfish men played their cards with cold-blooded efficiency. They were ardent collectors of tips, bribes, and valuable gifts. They had to be unscrupulous, ever suspicious, sharp-witted careerists to come out on top for a while in the turmoil and controversy following the harrowing decades after the Thirty Years' War. The "servants" of King Frederick William I were certainly not superior in intelligence or energy, let alone in forcefulness of personality to the early pioneers, but they had grown conscious of the burdensome proprieties of "Prussian Puritanism."

Although the nobles of descent continued to enjoy great initial advantage, their rise in the official hierarchy was often impeded or blocked by the successful competition of "immodest" commoners of some distinguishing personal quality. This trespassing on traditional class functions and monopolies and the ensuing rivalry between nobles and nonnobles were a notable phenomenon only in a little, though extremely important niche of the social order: in the realm of dynastic employment. Here, from the outset, a major problem presented itself, the problem of the compatibility of two coexistent, disparate social ladders of advancement.

In view of this situation, some *modus vivendi* had to be found between the antagonistic claims to social position which arose from the old, simple way of equating noble birth with superior social worth and personal excellence and the new, more individualized and more fluid practice of rating man on the basis of his vocational qualities, political utility, and official grade in the state service.

The ancient social rank order was regulated by inherited privilege, landownership, and genealogical considerations. The new service rank order was determined by office, function, and the will of the autocratic prince. In government employment, official position as a fountain of social esteem and self-respect competed with rank derived from exalted birth. Men of "poor extraction" frequently became the supervisory or commanding officers of old-established aristocrats.

This impertinent innovation, the growth of "unfair competition," gave rise to new and knotty relationships between nobles and commoners. Unabating irritation and friction were bound to emanate from the fact that the holding of significant posts under the authority of the crown became an important determinant of social status. In accordance with the novel yardstick for gauging merit and excellence, the upper service grades and the more imposing official titles *per se* became conspicuous symbols of high social standing. Thus organizational status, relative to hereditary prestige, gained vastly in significance as a social ranking device with the rise of the modern bureaucratic state.

BIBLIOGRAPHY

S. H. Aronson, *Status and Kinship in the Higher Civil Service,* Cambridge, Mass, 1964.

G. E. Aylmer, *The King's Servants,* New York, 1961.

S. N. Eisenstadt, *Political Systems of Empire,* New York, 1963.

L. Fallers, ed., *The King's Men,* New York, 1964.

Franklin L. Ford, *Robe & Sword: The Regrouping of the French Aristocracy After Louis XIV,* Cambridge, Mass, 1953.

M. Goehring, *Die Aemterkaeuflichkeit im Ancien Régime,* Berlin, 1938.

A. Goodwin, ed., *The European Nobility in the Eighteenth Century: Studies of the Nobilities of the Major European States in the Pre-Reform Era,* London, 1953.

THE BOURGEOIS WAY OF LIFE IN 18TH CENTURY FRANCE *

Elinor G. Barber

As this essay itself states, different social classes are always and everywhere identifiable by their different styles of life. Also, these different styles of life express the attitudes of the different social classes toward social mobility, as well as other aspects of social life. How the bourgeoisie and the nobility in 18th century France could be identified by different ways of life is vividly reported here. And how the bourgeoisie was ambivalent about the two possible ways of life, and why, is also carefully described.

Elinor G. Barber has taught at Smith College and the School of

* Reprinted from Elinor G. Barber, *The Bourgeoisie in 18th Century France,* Princeton: Princeton University Press, 1955.

General Studies, Columbia University. She is now Special Editor,
Biographies, of the forthcoming International Encyclopedia of the
Social Sciences.

In any society, different classes are identifiable by their different
ways of life. To the observer, that is, the many different kinds of
behavior that go on within the same society are symbolic of membership in one or another of the classes of which the society is made up.
The kinds of behavior that may be symbolically significant in this way
are innumerable, but a few examples of the more important ones will
indicate what patterns of activity are most often involved here: clothing,
speech, family life, education, an appropriate occupation, food, or recreation—all serve to symbolize membership in a particular social class,
apart from any other function they may have. The symbolic function
of occupations may be illustrated by recalling the prestige of a military
as compared to a mercantile career in pre-Revolutionary France; and
as for speech, the "Oxford accent" has traditionally been associated
with the English upper classes; in American society, the kind of car a
man drives or the kind of fur coat his wife wears are important guides
to social behavior. Even minimal clues tell us necessary things we need
to know in dealing with friends and especially with strangers. Veblen
may have thought that only the "leisure class" needed its symbols of
success, but we now know that the phenomenon of "conspicuous consumption," in this more generalized form, is common to all societies.

The behavior of a particular class will not only serve to identify
the class, but also it will be an expression of social attitudes. The class
system in its more dynamic aspect—the attitudes of the members of the
society toward social mobility—will be reflected in the styles of life of
the several classes, and especially in the differences between them. The
belief in the fundamental equality of all members of the society and
in their right to equality of opportunity will be expressed in a different
way in the styles of life from the disapproval of social mobility and
the hereditary segregation of functions. In American society, for example, differences in styles of dress are minimized, and only a sophisti-
cated eye can tell a dress from Gimbel's from one purchased at Bergdorf
Goodman's; and only the initiated know that while "everyone" has a
car, a DeSoto outranks a Chevrolet.[1] In the *ancien régime* in France,
which came nearer to being a caste society, distinctions were explicitly

---

[1] On this subject see B. Barber and L. Lobel, " 'Fashion' in Women's Clothes
and the American Social System," *Social Forces*, XXXI (Dec. 1952), pp. 124–131.

approved, and symbolic differentiation of dress was very clearly in evidence. Sometimes it was even confirmed by law, as in the case of the legally exclusive right of the nobility to wear both a sword and fur. Fabrics and even colors to be used in dress were allocated on the basis of class status.

Besides exemplifying class attitudes, styles of life also express religious values. They vary in accordance with religious definitions of right and proper conduct, with important convictions about the general worth-whileness of earthly goods and of earthly success, or about the purpose and significance of wealth or knowledge. The "this-worldly asceticism" of the wealthy Calvinist bourgeois affected his way of life in a different way from the religion of the wealthy Catholic; the latter could more easily segregate monastic asceticism from lay worldliness. In an integrated society, the religious and the social class attitudes will be congruent with one another; that is, they will not make conflicting demands on the individual; also, in an integrated society, any set of class attitudes will be internally consistent. For the mobile bourgeois of the 18th century, however, two kinds of conflict existed: a conflict between his attitudes as a bourgeois and his religious values, and also an ambivalence within his class attitudes toward social mobility.

The 18th century witnessed a considerable change in the ways of life of all the classes of France, a change which brought these conflicting pressures to bear on the bourgeois. Before the 18th century, the allocation of symbols of status was much more rigidly determined on the basis of the traditional class status of a particular family. During the 18th century men still reminisced about former times when "no bourgeois ever . . ." did thus and so. The nobility had formerly preempted luxurious living, artistic and literary cultivation, and, by the 17th century especially, a life that was predominantly idle. The functions traditionally allocated to the nobility—military and especially political—were now being filled by others, and so decorative idleness almost became synonymous with "vivre noblement." The bourgeoisie, on the other hand, was traditionally characterized by being hard-working, "sober," and frugal. But in the 18th century, the great increase in wealth among certain groups in the bourgeoisie increased the pressure that the socially ambitious bourgeois felt toward assimilation to the noble way of life by the manipulation of the various status-conferring symbols. More and more, the upper bourgeoisie, particularly, aimed at the acquisition of those symbols of noble status which came within its financial reach, while the middle bourgeoisie had rather more divided loyalties between the old bourgeois style of life and the noble style which was compatible with its mobility aspirations.

The ambivalences in the religious and class attitudes of the bourgeoisie that we have already discussed come clearly to the surface when we study the bourgeois way of life. To be a successful bourgeois at all meant making important compromises with the other-worldly orientation prescribed by the Catholic religion. These compromises the bourgeois businessman made. He shifted his attention to this world, and he assumed new responsibilities and set himself new goals. To carry out these new aims, it was only *rational,* of course, for the bourgeois to live simply. Luxurious consumption was incompatible with the financial demands of successful business operations and, further, such consumption too often ran the risk of inviting spoliation by the government. But in sober and frugal living the French bourgeois also found a way of easing the strain of his defection from traditional Catholic other-worldliness. The Church itself came to recognize the bourgeois's sober and conscientious devotion to his worldly affairs as a proper way to insure the salvation of his soul. For the bourgeois, the attainment of virtue came to be defined in terms of his ability to resist the worldly temptations of wealth.[2]

Far more than the Calvinist bourgeois, the French bourgeois came, ultimately, to compromise the moral and rational prescriptions for an ascetic way of life. The sober bourgeois was profoundly attracted by the noble way of life, and he was less deeply concerned with the problem of his salvation. Both the Calvinist and the Catholic bourgeois became more and more secularized, but while for the Calvinist this-worldly asceticism remained a driving force even in the secularized capitalist, the secularized French bourgeois shed his religious interests far more completely in his quest for social salvation in the form of nobility. The struggle that these French bourgeois experienced in the process of their secularization shows not only in their reflections about religion but in the ways they sought and symbolized social mobility. Once again, we find every bourgeois caught in the dilemma between acceptance of the traditional social and religious order, and rejection of that order insofar as it defined his place in it as fixed.

The fundamental problem of finding a way of life that was morally as well as socially acceptable was shared by all members of the mobile bourgeoisie, but there were variant solutions to this problem within the bourgeois class, and therefore different ways of life. The whole bour-

---

[2] Groethuysen, *Buergerliche Welt- und Lebensanschauung,* II, pp. 70, 76.

geois class shared, in fact, only one important pattern in its several ways of life, and that was its devotion to family life. To be sure, in the noble class, where the most important criterion of status was membership in a traditionally noble family, lineage and family connections were of great significance; and also, when the fief and other property became *de facto* hereditary, this connection of family and property increased the importance of children, and especially male children, to a noble father. But where the noble concern for the family had to do with pride and property, the bourgeois attitude constituted all this and more besides. To the bourgeois, domesticity or life *in the home* with his family had greater emotional significance than it did for the nobility. Physical well-being in the home was very important, and any threats to its physical safety were resented.[3] In bourgeois homes, harmony and affection between members of the family, between husbands and wives, and between parents and children, were ideals and reality. Man and wife "lived together and did not blush for it, while in the nobility man and wife pretended to live separately, at least in public." [4] From this emphasis on conjugal happiness it was only a step, made in the course of the Revolution, which brought the general acceptance of bourgeois values, to the identification of virtue with premarital chastity and marital fidelity. Glotz, in discussing the qualities of the hostesses of salons, speaks of their moral authority, which "in the 18th century . . . is not conferred by virtue in the sense of chastity. There was much talk of virtue at that time, but it meant disinterestedness and generosity, an eloquent concern for the public welfare. The word never had that narrow and somewhat overscrupulous sense that the 19th century gave it. One had to wait for the substitution of bourgeois for aristocratic morality before such a high price was attached to good morals, to respectability." [5] But even before the Revolution enthroned "middle class respectability," in all its aspects, the bourgeoisie disapproved of the lax sexual morality for which the 18th century nobility was famous.

Among the 18th century bourgeois, the older ideal of the stern parent changed to that of the loving, if not doting, parent. Friendship rather than authority relations developed between parents and children.[6] Vanel observes that whenever there were exceptions in Caen to the strict obedience relationship between parents and children, they

---

[3] Roustan, *Les philosophes*, pp. 233–234.
[4] Lacroix, *18ᵉ siècle*, p. 66.
[5] Marguerite Glotz, *Salons du 18ᵉ siècle* (Paris, 1945), pp. 14–15.
[6] Babeau, *Les bourgeois*, pp. 301–302.

occurred among the bourgeoisie.[7] Barbier revealed the association contemporaries made between close family ties and the bourgeois way of
life when he noted, in 1750, the welcome given by the king to two
of the royal princesses at Fontainebleau: "The king kissed them, first
one, then the other, for a quarter of an hour, crying *like a good Parisian
bourgeois head of the family*." [8] . . .

But the emphasis on family life was the *one* aspect of the bourgeois
way of life which cut across all its sub-groups, and as soon as we speak,
for example, of patterns of recreation and entertainment we touch on
areas in which the variations within the bourgeois class were immense.
The lawyer in a small town like Doué for whom recreation meant quiet
interfamily visiting, and the Parisian financier who required the most
lavish entertainment, lived in two different and hostile worlds, and
even among the Parisian bourgeoisie there were many styles of life.
These styles range along a continuum, from great simplicity and
austerity at one end to extreme luxury at the other, and the many
points on the continuum between the two extremes show the progressive compromises made by the mobile bourgeois between the "old"
bourgeois sobriety and the lure of the symbols of noble status.

The "old" bourgeoisie, composed of merchants, doctors, and lawyers,
were well-to-do if not wealthy people, whose way of life can be described by such terms as simplicity, sobriety, and industry. The frequent
designation of this group as *old* bourgeoisie derived from the fact that
both their social and economic status as bourgeois was of relatively long
standing, and was, therefore, in striking contrast to the status and
wealth of the financiers, who were, rightly or wrongly, generally
thought of as the "nouveaux riches." [9] This group held most tenaciously
to the old bourgeois style of life, to which, in part at least, it owed its
slow social rise. Their full approval was given to simple and frugal
living. Besnard wrote in his *Souvenirs* that in Doué in the mid-18th
century any luxury was entirely reserved for great seigneurs and a few
very wealthy merchants.[10] Barbier wrote approvingly about a M. de
Laverdy, a controller of finances: "Much has been said about M. de

---

[7] Vanel, *La vie publique à Caen*, p. 49.

[8] Barbier, *Journal*, III, pp. 176–177; our italics.

[9] The wealth of many financiers, e.g., the Boullongnes, was not really "new,"
but it increased so rapidly in a comparatively short period of time as to create that
impression. See Caix de Saint-Aymon, *Une famille d'artisan et de financiers du
17ᵉ et 18ᵉ siècle. Les Boullongnes* (Paris, 1914).

[10] Besnard, *Souvenirs*, I, p. 218.

Laverdy's frugality and modest living. He and his wife had an income of at most 16,000 livres. They lived piously and in the bourgeois manner; the ways of the Court did not suit them." [11] M. Grosley went so far as to call sobriety the very fountain of youth for both body and soul of the bourgeoisie.[12] . . .

Besides sobriety and austerity, thrift—the elimination of waste and the preoccupation with saving money—was another cardinal commandment of the bourgeois way of life. In part, this was an occupational necessity; it was "good business." The merchant could not "waste" excess income on luxurious consumption, but must add it to productive capital to expand the earning power of his enterprise. But the bourgeois felt that careful economy was more than just a rational prescription; it was also a moral duty and a way of indicating the fact that, for better or worse, a man *was* a bourgeois and had a serious and honest purpose in the world. Sombart sees this economy as one of the most important virtues peculiar to the bourgeois, "not thrift imposed by necessity, by want, but thrift conceived as a virtue." [13] Such thrift in the use of resources was the very opposite of the noble attitude toward his patrimony; the nobleman spent up to the hilt and tried only, as best he could, to keep out of debt. Séras felt that before there was ever any possibility of a *noblesse commerçante* in France (which he doubted, anyway) it would be necessary to convince the nobility of the necessary qualifications of the merchant: "One must not conceal from the nobility that vehement desires, the taste for frivolous amusements, are more harmful in the commercial occupation than in any other; for if on the one hand the activities of that occupation help to accumulate wealth, it demands on the other hand more restraint, precision, industry, economy, than any of those professions that the nobility can enter." The uncontrolled desires, Séras warned, would inevitably destroy what had been built up in the spirit of moderation.[14] The way of life of the proper bourgeois protected him from such disaster. The way in which the bourgeoisie was identified with thrift is amusingly illustrated in a remark by the lawyer Target, in 1787: "The state of our finances seems to be more disquieting than ever: but what remedy is there when on the occasion of some attempts by the King to economize in his own

[11] Barbier, *Journal*, IV, p. 480.

[12] Grosley, *Vie de M. Grosley* (Londres, 1787), p. 49.

[13] Werner Sombart, *Le bourgeois, contribution à l'histoire morale et intellectuelle de l'homme économique moderne* (Paris, 1926), p. 133.

[14] Séras, *Le commerce ennobli*, pp. 25-26.

household, it is said that *he acts like a bourgeois.*[15] This was evidently
no practice fit for a king of France.

The devotion of the man of the bourgeoisie to his work, which we
have mentioned earlier in connection with social values, constitutes
the third important component of the "old" bourgeois way of life. If
the work of the bourgeois was coordinated in some way with the attainment of salvation, it was, too, an end in itself, and it took precedence over
all other activities of this world. Even intellectual pursuits had only
the status of "avocations." The bourgeois of Dijon, for example, though
he might have a great interest in all kinds of studies, felt a much
higher obligation to his work. The driest studies, even, were considered
to be mere diversions. The well-known humanist Bouhier was always
a lawyer first and an author second.[16] The long, hard hours put in by
his lawyer colleagues, both young and old, were noted by Berryer,[17]
and Bachaumont quoted the following comment on his doctor-grand-
father by a jealous colleague: "He is a complete hypocrite, who will
do anything, provided he profits from it; a melancholy, burning man,
who talks only about the Virgin Mary and of scruples, and who, in
every possible way, seeks only to increase his practice and his fortune."[18] This is not an unfamiliar caricature of the bourgeois.

When we come, now, to consider the way of life of the middle
bourgeoisie more closely, we find that in addition to the traditional
moral pressure toward austerity, thrift, and industry, toward the interests of business and success as a bourgeois, there were also strong
pressures exerted on the mobile bourgeois away from this style of life.
"Vivre noblement" and all it implied pulled the French businessman,
more or less strongly, toward luxury, extravagance, and idleness. Those
who resisted these latter pressures to a large extent expressed strong
disapproval of the luxury-loving group, but by the 18th century few
escaped this kind of "corruption" altogether.

By the 18th century, the very strict rules on how "clothes varied
according to status" had been relaxed considerably. A hundred years
earlier, certain kinds of cloth were used exclusively by members of
certain classes: drugget by the artisan, woolen cloth by the bourgeois,
and silk by the nobility. In those days, women of the high bourgeoisie

[15] Boulloche, *Target,* p. 47.
[16] Bouchard, *La bourgeoisie bourguignonne,* p. 485.
[17] Berryer, *Souvenir,* I, pp. 33–34.
[18] Louis P. de Bachaumont, *Anecdotes piquantes pour servir à histoire de la
société française à la fin du règne de Louis XV* (Bruxelles, 1881), II, Appendix
"Jeunesse," pp. 229–230.

might wear taffeta, but velours were reserved for noblewomen.[19] These rigid distinctions were broken down by less conservative people in the 18th century, although Taine undoubtedly exaggerates the levelling that had taken place between the classes, and the extent of symbolization of egalitarian values in dress.[20] Black and grey were still the two colors used predominantly by the *roturiers* of Laval, though some wealthy bourgeois did use bright colors: "But the old bourgeois remained faithful during a large part of the 18th century to his dark colored dress. . . ."[21] The English traveller Arthur Young objected to the black clothes of persons of "moderate fortune" not so much because of the "dusky hue of this company," but "as too great a distinction"; and he thought that the "pride, arrogance and ill-temper of English wealth" would never have stood for it.[22]

French wealth also was becoming too "proud" for such humble clothing. At Doué, bright-colored hair ribbons and furbelows were worn not only by noblewomen but also by those "who by their markedly superior wealth or high profession of their husbands were distinguished from the other bourgeois families." However, wives of notaries, surgeons and retail merchants, that is, lesser bourgeois, did not permit themselves this luxury.[23] At Angers, the customs were on the whole the same, and bourgeois ladies over fifty who wore any colors were still subject to ridicule.[24] Little Manon Phlipon recalled that the bourgeois of Paris spent quite a lot of money to look his best on his Sunday afternoon walks in the Tuileries, or on such occasions as baptisms and weddings,[25] but unfortunately she did not compare this bourgeois finery with that of the nobility. The bourgeois always ran the risk of "overdressing" for his status, of meeting with censure and ridicule from his fellow-bourgeois or from the nobility. Mme. Tamisier must have been a well-dressed lady, judging by the inventory of her wardrobe, but she had been careful not to "parade a degree of luxury above that proper to her status.[26] Barbier's contempt for M. Dodun, who "had had a

[19] Vanel, *La vie publique à Caen*, p. 179.

[20] H. Taine, *Les origines de la France contemporaine. L'ancien régime* (Paris, 1898), pp. 407–408.

[21] J. M. Richard, *La vie privée dans une province de l'Ouest: Laval au 17ᵉ et 18ᵉ siècle* (Paris, 1922), p. 82.

[22] Arthur Young, *Travels in France and Italy during the Years 1787, 1788, and 1789* (London, Toronto, New York, 1915), p. 108.

[23] Besnard, *Souvenirs*, I, p. 28.

[24] *Ibid.*, I, p. 120.

[25] Roland, *Mémoires*, pp. 19–20.

[26] O. Teissier, *La maison d'un bourgeois au 18e siècle* (Paris, 1895), p. 15.

suit adorned with lace, no more and no less than that of an officer in the gendarmes," which was judged by all to be utterly ridiculous and made people dig up his lowly birth,[27] reveals the dangers and strains in the situation. . . .

Forms of address, both of parents and relatives, and of strangers and acquaintances, were differentiated by class in the *ancien régime,* and here too the bourgeois tried to acquire some of the appellations and titles of the noble.[28] Although the bourgeois were still given to nicknames (Jacquon, Pierrot, Manon, etc.) which were characteristic of the lower classes, they now used such expression as "mon chère père," and "ma chère mère," which were current only among the nobility and which were considered ludicrous by the artisans.[29] François Chéron recalled that his niece Marie was always "bourgeoisement" called Manette, because more elegant fashions in names were not yet current at the time.[30] Already by the 17th century, merchants in larger towns especially had acquired the title of "monsieur," even when spoken to by the nobility, instead of "maître," which was used only for artisans.[31] By the later 18th century, even women of the middle bourgeoisie of Ponthivy had ceased to sign modestly "La . . . une telle," and were now "Demoiselles." [32] The best-known ambition of the bourgeois, of course, was to acquire the *particule.* M. de Boulogne, a future *roturier* prelate, himself added this particle to his name, for no one with any ambition would dream of signing "simply Boulogne." [33] And the same ambitions prompted M. Geoffrion, a merchant of Valenciennes, to "polish up his only to evident status as *roturier* by adding to his name that of the fief of Volouris." [34]

The number of really elaborate bourgeois town houses was small in the 18th century. Besnard recalled that in Angers, in the latter half of the century, there was hardly a private home remarkable either for size or exterior appearance. The first one was built while he lived there.

[27] Barbier, *Chronique,* I, p. 379.

[28] Note that these bourgeois aspirations are a far cry from the revolutionary appellation of "citoyen," inspired by egalitarian ideals, and from the universal use of "mister" in American society.

[29] Besnard, *Souvenirs,* I, p. 56.

[30] Hervé-Bazin, "Récits inédits de François Chéron sur la vie de famille dans les classes bourgeoises avant la Révolution," *Revue de l'Anjou,* II (1881), p. 68.

[31] Babeau, *Les bourgeois,* pp. 73–74.

[32] F. L. Lay, *Histoire de la ville et communauté de Ponthivy au 18e siècle* (Paris, 1911), p. 48.

[33] Abbé Alphonse Delacroix, *M. de Boulogne, archévêque de Troyes* (Paris, 1886), p. 12.

[34] Legros, "Dépenses d'un bourgeois," pp. 212–213.

Even the wealthiest families lived in relatively small houses and crowded several beds into one room. In Doué, where he lived in his youth, there were only two "better" homes, which were distinguished by greater elegance and cleanliness.[35] At Troyes, though, and also at Dijon, the richest merchants did build huge houses. At Marseilles the Borelli had such a house, at Bordeaux the wine merchant Bethman, and at Abbeville the Van Robais.[36] And the wealthiest financiers, as we shall see, laid a very high premium on the building of magnificent mansions. But even the modest-living old bourgeois had one luxury very close to his heart when it came to housing, and this was a country house.[37] A great many of the bourgeois families at Doué had country houses and "châteaux" at a greater or lesser distance from town, and they hastened to go there whenever business permitted. On holidays, the town became a desert.[38] The men of the time loved nature; their country homes were simply furnished, and general informality was customary there. Also, of course, it was the fashion to go to the country, and the bourgeois no longer ignored such "fashions." [39]

For the middle bourgeois, however, the gradual adaptation to a more luxurious way of life concomitant with upward mobility was problematic, and he had some guilt feelings about it. It was perhaps because of these very guilt feelings that the middle bourgeois reacted so negatively to the luxurious living of the financial bourgeoisie who had no apparent hesitations about extravagance and luxury. . . .

It was *nouveau-riche* presumption rather than just luxury that Barbier was attacking here, though great luxury itself was often shocking and outrageous to the "bon bourgeois." M. Hardy, the old-fashioned gentleman mentioned before, was full of shocked disapproval, for example, at a bourgeois wedding carried out in great style: "In order to transmit to posterity an example of the ostentation of the bourgeoisie of this century, I thought I had better insert here a small detail about the crazy expenditures made on the occasion of the marriage celebrated here today between . . . the oldest son of sieur Trudon, a dealer in groceries who has in the village of Antony, near Paris, a famous candle factory, and who lives in Paris, and Mlle. Jouanne. . . ." Hardy remarked that the girl's dowry was 80,000 livres; he catalogued all her expensive gifts and described the elegance of the wedding banquet,

[35] Besnard, *Souvenirs*, I, pp. 119, 14.
[36] Babeau, *Les bourgeois*, p. 55ff.
[37] Vanel, *La vie publique à Caen*, p. 113.
[38] Besnard, *Souvenirs*, I, p. 127.
[39] Babeau, *Les bourgeois*, p. 213ff.

comparing it to one held at the marriage of none less than the Duke of Chartres to Mlle. de Penthièvre.[40] Even Mme. d'Epinay, brought up in a fairly well-to-do bourgeois home, was shocked when she first came to Epinay and found "all that the most refined, and I dare say the most indecent luxury might conceive of in the way of useless and nevertheless pleasant things."[41] . . .

Of all the bourgeois of the *ancien régime*, none made greater or, on the whole, more successful efforts to assimilate to the noble style of life than did the very wealthy Parisian financiers and a few of the most famous Parisian lawyers, though even in the provinces there were high-living merchants. These bourgeois had, apparently, no scruples about social pretension; their attitudes toward luxury were quite different from the hesitant steps toward gracious living that crept into the way of life of the old bourgeoisie. The old bourgeoisie shared the hostility and contempt of the nobility for these *nouveaux riches,* who spent their new wealth in the lavish manner of the noble class, but often with a lack of aesthetic discrimination or "taste" that laid them open to ridicule. . . .

The 18th century financiers had almost a craze for building palatial mansions and châteaux, and there was not one of them with whom one or more magnificent residences in Paris or its environs could not be associated. Most of this building occurred between 1730 and 1780, and many of the suburban estates were so fine that they were acquired by the wealthy nobility after the decline of the financiers. Le Bas de Montargis' place at Venves went to no less a noble than Condé, Bernard's at Passy to Boulainvilliers, and Crozat's at Montmorency to the Comte de Luxembourg.[42] Furthermore, besides their interest in building, both the financiers and lesser bourgeois established themselves on these estates for the sake of landownership itself. Ever since the *ordonnance de Blois* in 1579, a *roturier* buying a noble fief could not simply purchase nobility along with it.[43] Except in various outlying provinces which had come late into the monarchy or enjoyed special laws—like Dauphiné, Béarn, and Provence—nobility was *personal* rather than *real*. But even so, and quite apart from the fact that landownership was often a very good financial investment, the bourgeois who aspired to nobility also still felt land to be an essential social investment. Land-

[40] Hardy, *Mes loisirs,* p. 142.

[41] D'Epinay, *Mémoires,* p. 322.

[42] Thirion, *La vie privée des financiers,* p. 313.

[43] M. Marion, *Dictionnaire des institutions de la France au 17e et 18e siècle* (Paris, 1923), p. 395.

ownership was the supreme symbol of the noble style of life, and ennoblement by other means was felt to be incomplete without it. . . .

While the greatest degree of luxury is rightly associated with the financiers, it is worth noting that some of the most successful lawyers in Paris lived in the style of great *seigneurs,* as did also many of the younger members of the traditionally more sober *robe.* Eminent lawyers like Gerbier, or Le Normand, whom we have already mentioned, had completely abandoned the sobriety of most of the members of the bar. Le Normand was "a great seigneur of a lawyer, magnificent in the kind of house he had, the kind of furniture and carriages; he was even more so in his country residence, where he received during the holidays men of high dignity, intellectuals, artists, and his most illustrious colleagues. This style of life, new for a lawyer, made the young members of the bar lose the simple ways of the old." [44] And of Gerbier it is said that he was "sumptuous in his living and worried little about his expenses." [45] At the very top of the professional bourgeoisie, then, the breach with the old ways was sometimes made, but it seemed even less compatible with professional dignity than the luxury of the business elite. Barbier lamented that the abandoning of long black robes by the legal profession detracted from its dignity in the public eye.[46]

Among the wildly extravagant and luxury-loving financiers, there were the classic examples of the absurdly ill-at-ease and miscast *nouveaux riches,* and there were also financiers who easily outdid the nobility in their intellectual and aesthetic sophistication. Manon Phlipon, at the age of eighteen, visited one of the former kind of financiers, the rich son of a *fermier-général,* and she commented that "the caricature of good taste produced here a kind of elegance foreign alike to bourgeois simplicity and to artistic taste. . . . It was worse with the men: the sword of the master of the house, the efforts of the chef . . . could not compensate for the awkwardness of their manners, the deficiencies of language when they wanted to make it seem distinguished, or the commonness of their expressions when they forgot to watch themselves." [47] And there were many others, who were simply rich, spoke badly, and were little read, and who were "the first to laugh at their own ignorance or their solecisms, which, anyway, never kept anyone away from their excellent dinners and their splendid recep-

[44] Gaudry, *Histoire du barreau,* II, p. 92.
[45] *Ibid.,* II, p. 174.
[46] Barbier, *Journal,* II, p. 346.
[47] Roland, *Mémoires,* p. 97ff.

tions." [48] Beaujon, the court banker, for example, was among those "Turcarets" or "bourgeois gentilshommes," whom, according to Campan, one saw "with a confidence not general with commoners, pronounce impressive words empty of sense, judge without knowing anything about the subject, and brag about their good fortunes." [49] Campan, in fact, preferred the simple, crude, old-style financier to the second generation, which acquired nothing but pride and pretensions and a snobbish contempt for its *roturier* parents.[50]

But more remarkable, perhaps, than the fact that some financiers were uncultivated and pretentious boors, is the large number of these wealthy men who sought to exhibit something more than what Veblen calls "pecuniary ability," who did strive for literary and artistic appreciation, and, in some cases even, performance. They were the new patrons of arts and letters, and as the sponsors of "high-brow" entertainment they also participated in intellectual activities. Grimm wrote that it was ridiculous to accuse these mid-18th century financiers of being mere Turcarets; such men as Caze, de la Porte de Sénancourt, or Grimod Dufort and Lantage de Félicourt were polished men of society.[51] One of these elegant and cultivated financiers was Dupin de Franceuil, one-time lover of Mme. d'Epinay, who taught her much about the world of the salons, both about their rituals and their culture. Helvetius retired from the *fermes* to devote himself to writing, and Lavoisier, the scientist, was an ex-financier. La Popelinière tried his hand at writing, less successfully. Le Normand de Tournehem, La Live de Bellegarde, and Grimod de la Reynière, all collected philosophers and artists around them. Pierre Crozat was a really great art collector, one of a dynasty of Crozats who devotedly and intelligently patronized the arts.[52] His collection of Italian art was really good, and Mariette, one of the greatest art experts of the time, was very much impressed when he catalogued it after Crozat's death in 1743.[53] La Reynière was a genuine lover of music, and gave very enjoyable concerts at his home.[54] Chevrier, too, admitted that these financiers were cultivated men " 'who create the delight of a chosen society, by the

[48] Thirion, *La vie privée des financiers*, p. 263.
[49] Campan, *Le mot et la chose* (s.l., 1751), p. 67.
[50] *Ibid.*, p. 65ff.
[51] Roustan, *Les philosophes*, p. 179 ff.
[52] Thirion, *La vie privée des financiers*, p. 42.
[53] A. de Janzé, *Les financiers d'autrefois; fermiers généraux* (Paris, 1886?), p. 62.
[54] *Ibid.*, p. 235.

pleasures of an elaborate imagination and the charms of a pleasant disposition.' " [55]

By now it must be clearly evident that the bourgeois way of life as a whole, and the differences and changes within it, were closely tied in with the attitudes of the bourgeois toward social mobility. It reflects the conflict between the acceptance of the traditional hereditary class patterning of styles of life, and the desire of the bourgeoisie to rise to the prestigious and esteemed noble pattern of living. More or less, almost all the bourgeois sought the symbols of the noble style of life; more or less they sought to abandon the old bourgeois way of living and to slough off the stigma of their *roture*. The different degrees of change in the way of life of the bourgeoisie are indicative of the conflicts experienced by this class in their quest for mobility.

BIBLIOGRAPHY

Elizabeth Baldwin, *Sumptuary Legislation and Personal Regulation in England*, Johns Hopkins University Studies in History and Political Science, 1926.

Bernhard Groethuysen, *Die Entstehung der Buergerlichen Welt- und Lebensanschauung in Frankreich*, 2 vols., Halle, 1927–1930.

Georges Lefebvre, *The Coming of the French Revolution*, trans. by R. R. Palmer, Princeton, 1947.

W. E. Minchinton, "The Merchants in England in the Eighteenth Century," *Explorations in Entrepreneurial History*, X (1957), 62–71.

[55] Quoted in Frederick C. Green, *La peinture des moeurs de la bonne société dans le roman français de 1715 à 1761* (Paris, 1924), pp. 242–243.

SOCIAL MOBILITY AMONG THE SERVANT CLASS OF 18TH CENTURY ENGLAND *

J. Jean Hecht

In the literature about social stratification, until quite recent times, there has been relatively much less written about the lower than the

* Reprinted from J. Jean Hecht, *The Domestic Servant Class in Eighteenth-Century England*, London: Routledge & Kegan Paul Ltd., 1956. By permission.

upper social classes. One group of comparatively lower class people about whom we do know a certain amount are servants, people who worked for the middle and upper classes and who were much discussed by their employers. Hecht has collected a great deal of valuable information about the servants in eighteenth century England and here discusses the amounts, degrees, and channels of social mobility that characterized this group, a group that constituted one of the largest occupational categories of the time.

J. Jean Hecht has taught at New York University and Smith College. He is on the Executive Committee of the Conference of British Studies. He is presently at work on a study of the aristocratic family in eighteenth century England.

If service could mean a comfortable and protected existence, and an opportunity to acquire a competence, it also functioned as a path for social ascent. Many who enlisted in its ranks were thereby enabled to improve their social status, some rising a few degrees in the social scale, others radically altering their condition.

I

In order to trace the process of ascension it is necessary to define the standing of service as an occupation. The limitations of the available material and the presence of certain ambiguities in the hierarchy of occupations itself make it impossible to do this with precision, but it can be done in a general way.

Enough contemporary comment has survived to indicate that, on the whole, service was considered a somewhat demeaning occupation. A certain stigma attached to much of the servant class. The readiness with which both men and women became domestics, however, testifies to the stigma's mildness. So, too, does the general tone of the group. There appears to have been none of the gloomy discontent, none of the acute sense of degradation or personal indignity so common among servants in more recent times.[1] Austin, who visited England in the opening years of the nineteenth century, observed of the London footmen: ". . . these people wear the appearance of the most perfect contentment. They are

[1] For the attitude of the twentieth-century domestic toward service see Violet M. Firth, *The Psychology of the Servant Problem*, [1925,] pp. 18–19, 21, 31–2; *The Report of the Committee Appointed to Enquire into the Present Condition as to the Supply of Female Domestic Servants*, pp. 15–16; Elaine Burton, *Domestic Work*, [1944,] p. 4.

pleased with their party coloured clothes, and never seem more happy than when they expose themselves to the public." [2] And Silliman, who came a few years later, commented with surprise on the complacency of servants in general. "In England," he wrote, "the servant is contented with his condition." [3] Had these American travellers come fifty or a hundred years earlier, they undoubtedly would have carried away the same impression. But, however mild it may have been, a stigma did exist.

It derived, in part, from the nature of the servant's social role. The real or imagined importance of an occupation for the subsistence and survival of the society in which it exists is one of the factors responsible for its standing. [4] In eighteenth-century England servants were looked upon as valueless to the community, as people who contributed little or nothing to the common welfare. This view was given expression time and again in the incidental remarks of writers concerned with divers subjects. In 1767 Nathaniel Forster called attention to "the numbers of servants . . . of both sexes entertained in gentlemen's families; who consume without mercy the produce of the state, with very little return of advantageous labour. . . ." [5] Terming the whole class "an unnecessary set of people in their present capacity," a "Yorkshire Tradesman" pointed out in 1772 that they "might be made very useful in other stations in life." [6] And in 1784 another writer referred to them "as drones in the hive, consuming the produce of others' labour and industry without contributing anything thereto. . . ." [7] As the most conspicuously idle of domestics, livery servants were sometimes singled out for comment. In 1743, for example, a contributor to the *Champion* voiced regret at finding so many husky young men living the unproductive life of a footman:

When I see four or five able Fellows swinging behind a gilt Chariot, and reflect, that they have no other Business to do that what, perhaps, might be better undone; that they are . . . of so little Use to Society, that in the

[2] Austin, *Letters from London*, p. 274.
[3] Silliman, *Journal of Travels*, I, 87.
[4] Kingsley Davis and Wilbert E. Moore, "Some Principles of Stratification," *American Sociological Review*, 1945, X. 243–4; Pitirim A. Sorokin, *Social Mobility*, New York and London, 1927, p. 100.
[5] [Nathaniel Forster,] *An Enquiry into the Causes of the Present High Price of Provisions*, 1767, p. 45.
[6] *London Chronicle*, 1772, XXXI. 421c.
[7] *Heads of a Plan*, p. 47. Cf. *London Chronicle*, 1766, XX. 560b; *An Address to the Gentry of the County of Durham*, Newcastle, 1779, pp. 19–20; [John Gray,] *A Plan for Finally Settling the Government of Ireland*, 1785, p. 20; *Manufactures Improper Subjects of Taxation*, p. 12.

Course of their whole Lives not one of them adds a *Shilling* to the publick *Stock,* I am grieved to see *Englishmen* in such a Situation.[8]

This being the general attitude, servants naturally enjoyed anything but a high repute.

Another source of the stigma they bore was the generally accepted theory of the relationship of master and servant. The servant, as has been shown, was viewed as a person who had temporarily relinquished his freedom; his position was conceived to be but a step or two removed from serfdom. In consequence, there attached to him at least a modicum of the ignominy that invariably attaches to the unfree. Thus the author of the piece in the *Champion* quoted above maintained that servants were "so far Slaves, as to make a part of the Equipage of their Masters. . . ." [9] And a newspaper correspondent in 1757 roundly declared: "I consider an Englishman in Livery, as a kind of Monster. He is a Person born free, with the obvious Badge of Servility, and I should think myself in better Company with the Farmer's Servant who buys his own Clothes. . . ." [10] An interesting rejoinder to these remarks, signed "R. D." and almost certainly by Robert Dodsley,[11] appeared in the same newspaper later in the year. The writer argues that "the Necessity of the subordinate Ranks, Conditions, and Offices of Men, sufficiently obviates the Dishonour and Disgrace of Servitude." Yet he reluctantly admits that "a Livery Suit may indeed fitly be called a Badge of Servility." [12]

A great many servants, however, entirely escaped the stigma. Those who served the nobility and the gentry were free of all taint. This is made quite clear by Hanway when he writes: ". . . I do not think that the Domestic in a *private livery,* is equal in office to a *husbandman* or a *mechanic.* On the other hand, the servant who is near the person of a Nobleman, or a Gentleman, . . . derives an importance from it which renders him respectable. . . ." [13]

The respectability of such servants was mirrored in their bearing towards those engaged in other occupations. They had neither the humility nor the diffidence normally characteristic of a despised group; rather, their manner was uniformly haughty, and their actions were often

---

[8] Quoted in *Gentleman's Magazine,* 1743, XIII. 433. Cf. *Lloyd's Evening Post,* 1780, XLVI. 307c; [John Feltham,] *A Picture of London for 1803,* 1803, pp. 273–4.

[9] Quoted in *Gentleman's Magazine,* 1743, XIII. 433.

[10] *London Chronicle,* 1757, II. 468c.

[11] Ralph Straus, *Robert Dodsley,* 1910, p. 388.

[12] *London Chronicle,* 1757, II. 612c.

[13] Hanway, *Eight Letters,* p. 59. Cf. *London Chronicle,* 1765, XVII. 459a.

insolent in the extreme. ". . . we find them," says an anonymous author, "so puffed up with Pride and Insolence, that it is no uncommon thing to see a good Tradesman, nay, sometimes People of Superior Rank, cringing to a saucy Lacky. . . ." [14] A satirical essay entitled *Below Stairs,* which was published in 1792, effectively reproduces their lofty attitude. Speaking of a grocer, a lady's maid says in Slipslop manner: "Such low people are beneath our attention; though some of them have the *frontery* to put themselves upon a footing with a nobleman's attendant, or a gentleman's servant." And she continues by remarking:

We sometimes condescend indeed to talk with them in familiar terms, as if they were our equals, and this has encouraged them to be arrogant. That enormous mass of a woman, our butcher's wife in St. James's market, accosts me with as much freedom, and as little *emberassment* as if she had belonged to a family of rank as well as myself. But I always discountenance such people and convince them that I know how to support the *spear* of life to which my stars have elevated me.[15]

To be sure, much of this hauteur originated in the servant's close identification with the social status of his employer, a fact with which contemporary observers were fully cognizant. A writer discoursing in 1767 on "The insolence . . . so much complained of among noblemen's servants" asserted: ". . . a consciousness of the dignity of the noble personage they serve . . . naturally make[s] them arrogant and proud." [16] And in 1782 the perceptive Vicesimus Knox saw their conduct in the same light: "They assume a share of the grandeur from the rank of their masters, and think themselves intitled to domineer over their equals, and to ridicule their superiors." [17] But equally important as a cause of their arrogance. was the prestige that the social status of their employers conferred upon them in the eyes of the general public. They were proud because they were respected.

The quantum of respect naturally varied with the nominal rank of the domestic. The duke's valet was held in greater esteem than his footman. Among the servants employed by the middle classes the same sort of variations prevailed.

In the hierarchy of occupations, then, service stood neither wholly

---

[14] *An Enquiry into the Melancholy Circumstances of Great Britain,* p. 21. Cf. [John Corry,] *A Satirical Review of London at the Commencement of the Nineteenth Century,* 1801, p. 79.

[15] *Carlton House Magazine,* 1792, I. 163.

[16] *Court Miscellany,* 1767, III. 413.

[17] *London Chronicle,* 1782, LII. 287a.

above nor wholly below such employments as keeping a shop or working as an artisan. There was considerable overlapping. While, as Hanway observed, the social status of the lower domestics who served the nobility and gentry was superior to that of the mechanic and the servant or labourer in husbandry, the social status of the lower domestics in middle-class families was not. Again, while the social status of the upper servants employed by the nobility and gentry was superior to that of the small tradesman, the social status of those employed by the middle classes probably was not.

II

From the foregoing analysis it is apparent that in itself entrance into service might or might not bring an improvement in social status, depending chiefly on the provenance of the servant, his nominal rank, and the social status of his employer. The clergyman's widow or the merchant's daughter whom circumstances forced to serve as housekeeper in a middle-class family suffered a distinct loss of prestige. On the other hand, the girl from the parish poorhouse who became a maid in a tradesman's home and the farmer's son who became footman to a duke undoubtedly improved their condition.

The domestic's initial place did not necessarily fix his social status for the duration of his career in service. He could rise by receiving promotion in the family in which he served or by exchanging his employer for one more elevated in the social scale.

Promotion was frequently given in order to fill a vacant post; it was often the easiest method of securing a servant with the experience that was necessary for so many household offices. A domestic might learn outside of service how to discharge the mechanical part of his duties, but practice was often the only way he could perfect himself in the elaborate system of forms that had to be observed when those duties were carried out. Ineptitude would imply that his master could not afford to engage a well-trained servant; that is, it would argue an inability to pay for the consumption of time and effort required for the preparation of such a servitor. More often than not, then, the awkward servant was wholly unacceptable. A letter written by Mrs. Montagu in 1745 perfectly illustrates the impatience with which his deficiencies were likely to be regarded. "The servant I part with," she explains, "is very honest, but I cannot bring him to deliver his sincerity in such delicate terms as are necessary in a message. He told a lady of quality who inquired after my health, that I was *pure stout,* and if I am in good spirits he tells people I am *brave.* . . ."[18] To avoid such maladroitness the common practice was to choose some servant who was already a member of the staff, train him for the post to be filled and then, after a brief novitiate, advance him permanently to that position.

Such preferment was also customarily given as a reward for satisfactory and extended service. The servant who acquitted himself well over a period of years was likely to be advanced to a higher post. Had it been otherwise, during the controversy over vails Hanway could hardly have named "greater *promotion*" as one of the compensatory benefits domestics would probably receive if those gratuities were abolished.[19]

A single promotion might raise a servant several degrees in the scale of rank. In giving an account of Elizabeth Chudleigh's domestic machinations after her marriage to the Duke of Kingston, Thomas Whitehead, who was at one time His Grace's valet, presents a number of examples. He tells how Thomas Philips, the butler, was made steward of one of the Duke's estates; how Williams, a footman, was raised to the position of butler; how one Dicks, who had been a gardener, was made a bailiff.[20]

Transitions such as that of Williams, from the lower ranks of the hierarchy to the upper, were not unusual. A mock petition purporting to have been drawn up by a group of waiting-women who sought the right to be styled "ladies," just as valets were called "gentlemen," plaintively observed: "The most pitiful, paltry, insignificant fellows in being, can get a Livery on their backs; and by a subordinate obedience, some insinuation, and great compliance, do very often get themselves promoted to the second table out of livery. . . ."[21] An essay in a series entitled the *Whimsical Philosopher* confirms this observation. Describing how the nobility and gentry chose their servants in medieval times, it asserts approvingly: "No fawning or pimping footman could then expect to become an upper servant in a great family. . . ."[22] The implied contrast with the eighteenth century is, of course, unmistakable. Further confirmation is supplied by the highly critical remarks of a newspaper correspondent who signed himself "Clytus." He assails the practice of "setting some minion to the government of the house, brought

[18] *Elizabeth Montagu,* I. 225.
[19] Hanway, *Sentiments and Advice of Thomas Trueman,* p. 30. [A "vail" is a gratuity or tip. The Editor.]
[20] Whitehead, *Original Anecdotes,* pp. 79, 159, 171.
[21] *London Chronicle,* 1765, XVII. 434b. Cf. *ibid.,* 1760, VII. 196b.
[22] *London Magazine,* 1750, XIX. 557.

from the most servile drudgery, and without the least education, more than barely writing his name." How is it possible, he asks,

to suppose such a person, assisted by a female . . . who never studied anything beyond the use of the mop and duster (set aside airs and impertinence) should be able to dispose a family of thirty, forty or fifty servants, in that good order which should redound honour and give a grace to dignity.

The badness of upper servants, he contends, is due largely to the fact that they are frequently persons who have been promoted from the lower staff; and he comments with surprise "that these promotions are rewards of a disposition which all gentlemen seem to hold in the utmost contempt." [23]

The promotion that elevated a servant to the upper staff sometimes came after he had risen by slow stages through the ranks of the lower household; sometimes, too, it proved but the prelude to further advancement. In fact, it was by no means uncommon for a servant who remained in the same family for a considerable time to rise gradually from a lowly office to one of the most exalted in the hierarchy. The case of Nancy Bere is typical. Taken from the local poorhouse by the Hackmans of Lymington to be a weeder in their garden, Nancy Bere was later employed by them as a kitchen maid. She evidently discharged her duties in that capacity satisfactorily; for in time Mrs. Hackman preferred her to the post of lady's maid, having first "had her carefully instructed in all the elementary branches of education." [24] Very similar was the ascent of a boy employed in the establishment of the younger Pitt. Beginning his rise as a helper in the stables, he was next made under-groom, then "taken to town to wait on the upper servants," "afterwards made a footman," and eventually promoted to the post of valet.[25] A news item published in 1757 mentions yet another case of the same order: the rise of a stable boy "in a certain Nobleman's Service" to the office of butler.[26]

Even the position of land steward, as John Mordant makes clear, was frequently attained by servants who rose in this manner. Discussing some of the errors into which the owners of estates commonly fall, Mordant cautions against "that of advancing *menial servants to the*

[23] *London Chronicle,* 1765, XVII. 459ab.
[24] Warner, *Literary Recollections,* I. 48–9.
[25] R[obert] Chambers, *The Book of Days,* 1864, I. 155–6.
[26] *London Chronicle,* 1757, I. 298a.

office of steward, that are not duly qualified. . . . "He then proceeds to give what purports to be an actual instance of such advancement:

There was a postillion advanced to the office of steward in the following manner. While in this low situation he behaved well, learned his A. B. C. of the *butler,* who also taught him to write his name, and in a little time could do so tolerably well, nay, in time he wrote a print hand so well as to be able to ticket the casks in the cellar: after some time he was made coachman, could cut the figure of 8 in smacking his whip and by a certain motion, or rather spring of it, would take a straw out of a dirt wall three times together, and not miss; nay, even when upon the coach box, and full speed, could by the elasticity of a certain whip of his own projecting, take up a fowl, or almost anything within its reach. In this situation he continued some years, drove with a great deal of care, improved himself in *letters,* could write a bill of his outgoings, and make a sum total, give a discharge upon receipt of it, speak good horse language, and had some notion of speaking well to the *pointers,* would curse the postillion with an *air,* and gave the wheel-horses the pretty names of *Gooseberry* and *Hard-arse;* when he gave them the whip upon the rump, would fetch the guttural sound of hoay, hoay, up the rough artery, as if his lungs was a curtal bag: he set his hat well, swore upon a proper accent. In short, he performed everything with propriety, and an uncommon gracefulness, would turn off a horn of October, and give a genteel hem after it; and at watering, &c. would whistle a horse till he drank or pissed to some tune. . . . In fine, he behaved so well, that he merited so much good will of his *lady,* that one day, John, says she, I have often thought of advancing thee, and as often mentioned it to your ——. Here is Mr. —— the steward of the —— estate, is almost superannuated and no *son* to succeed him, what think you of that——? replies John, with his wonted modesty, M—m, I have thought of such a thing; but then thought it too great a favour to ask, but M—m, it is what I could do perhaps as well as another, and if I should be so fortunate as to succeed, your *ladyship* may depend upon my utmost endeavours in that capacity also. John succeeds (Mr. ——) marries the housekeeper, and as soon as possible takes three or four hundreds a year of the *best* land in the lordship into his own hands, buys horses for his —— and most of the nobility and gentry in that part of the country; his wife brings him an only daughter, who is brought up at a French school, dances very fine, and plays as fine as any young *lady* on the spinet, &c. makes a grand appearance at the horse-race and assizes, as genteel as Miss —— And John and Madam on a winter evening by the parlour fire often talk (*if it could be brought about*) to marry Miss with *Master* —— the *counsellor.*[27]

[27] Mordant, *Complete Steward,* I. 208–10.

Manifestly this is satire, yet it is no less convincing as evidence than if it were an actual case history; for Mordant would scarcely have written it if employers had not been in the habit of preferring to the post of steward servants who, starting from the lower ranks, had risen through the *cursus honorum*.

A passage in the diary of the Rev. William Jones, written in 1800 but outlining events that had taken place some time earlier, describes the upward progress of such a servant:

A few years ago this great mushroom-man [Rogers] began his career in Lord Monson's stables. I had heard it frequently declared, but could hardly believe it, on account of his affected consequence, till Mrs. Shuldham, a most amiable lady, a relative of the Monson family, assured me it was truth. By degrees he worked himself into the house, &, in the absence of the *great* family, he had charge of the *great* house, which I suppose inspired him with *great* ideas. . . . Rogers had continued in the house so long & tasted so many sweets arising from the house, that he almost seemed to dream that the whole was his own. . . .

On the death of Mr. Parkinson, the Steward, a very honest, worthy man . . . Rogers started up into a great, a very great man; for he now received the rents.[28]

The picture certainly differs little in essentials from that presented by Mordant.

A servant might be helped, similarly, by the paternalism of his employer to transfer his services to an employer of higher social status. As a rule the aid a servant received in making a change of that sort was confined to the usual written or verbal character: he secured the place through his own efforts. Thomas Whitehead's account of how he became valet to the Duke of Kingston illustrates the point. While in the service of Sir Henry Oxenden, a country gentleman, he decided to look for a more advantageous position. ". . . accordingly," he writes,

I gave him warning, telling him I thought I might at my age, do better for myself in London; and hoped he would not be my hindrance. . . . Soon afterwards I was informed that the Duke of Kingston wanted a travelling valet. This news pleased me much: I thought, if I could get into a Duke's service, I should be provided for, for life. I mentioned it to my worthy mas-

---

[28] *The Diary of the Revd. William Jones, 1777–1821*, ed. O[ctavius] F. Christie, 1929, pp. 115–16.

ter, who gave me a letter of recommendation to his Grace, which I lost no time in taking to the Duke.[29]

By leaving the household of a country gentleman for that of a duke Whitehead improved his social status. He appears to have been chiefly concerned with the material benefits the change would bring, but he must also have been aware that it would increase his prestige.

Two servants employed at different times by the Rev. Woodforde altered their social status in much the same way. In 1784 his maid Lizzy, having been recommended by him, left his service to join the household of the local squire.[30] Again, in 1793 his footboy, whom he described as "being too big for his present place and deserving of a better," was taken on by the squire's brother.[31] In both instances the servant gained prestige by passing from the employ of a lesser man to that of a greater. But the footboy's social status may also have been improved in another way. From Woodforde's remark about his having outgrown his place, it seems likely that his new position may have been of a higher nominal rank than his old one: in changing places he may have received promotion.

Such promotions were probably not uncommon. It is reasonable to suppose that the servant who sought to better himself by changing places tried to capitalize to the full the training and experience he had acquired in his last position. Mandeville affirms the existence of such a tendency. "Ask for a Footman that for some time has been in Gentlemens Families," he says, "and you'll get a dozen that are all Butlers." [32]

But whether or not it entailed a rise in the hierarchy of rank, the transit of a servant from one employer to another higher in the social scale might be followed later on by several similar removes. A succession of changes might be a series of upward steps.

A change of places did not always bring social advancement. Just as a domestic might pass from the service of a middle-class employer to that of a gentleman or from the service of a gentleman to that of a nobleman, so he might move in the opposite direction, sinking in the social scale. Sally Gunton, for instance, after a term of service with the Townshends, one of the most eminent families of the Norfolk squire-

[29] Whitehead, *Original Anecdotes,* pp. 126–7.
[30] *Diary of a Country Parson,* II. 142.
[31] *Ibid.,* IV. 1, 3.
[32] Mandeville, *Fable of the Bees,* p. 345.

archy, went to live with the Rev. Woodforde.[33] And in the course of his career as a servant John Macdonald made at least two such changes. After serving Maj. Deibbiege, a gentleman, he entered the employ of Charles Ferguson, a wine merchant; and after living with Sir John Stuart of Allan Bank, he became footman to another wine merchant, James O'Neil.[34]

During a career of service changes of this kind might alternate with changes of the opposite order, the domestic's social status rising or falling with each new place. Macdonald, for example, moved back and forth between middle- and upper-class employers.[35]

Such a course stood in sharp contrast to the sort in which every change of place was a step in social advancement. Just how common either type was remains a matter of conjecture; both were possible lines that a servant's career might follow.

III

A career of service might lead to social advancement in other ways than through promotion and change of place. It might enable a servant to secure some employment or set up in some business that ranked above service in the hierarchy of occupations, or entitle him to a greater degree of respect than he had received before he entered service; it might even bring him financial independence.

The occupations that domestics entered on quitting service varied greatly. Sally Bussy, who had served Dr. Francis, father of Sir Philip Francis, became the landlady of a genteel lodginghouse.[36] Thomas Knowles, who had lived in the capacity of coachman to a Miss Clayton of Liverpool, set up as a brushmaker, selling both wholesale and retail.[37] Mrs. Delany's footman Richard went into the grocery business.[38] Hossack, the Earl of Egmont's valet, took up the practice of medicine and later wrote "a book on the mechanism of human bodies"; Henekin, another of his servants, left his employ "to study physic." [39] Adam

[33] *Diary of a Country Parson*, IV. 153.
[34] *Memoirs of an Eighteenth–Century Footman*, pp. 70–1, 238.
[35] *Ibid.*, introd., p. xvii and *passim*.
[36] *The Francis Letters*, ed. Beata Francis and Eliza Keary, 1901, I. 172–3.
[37] Richard Brooke, *Liverpool during the Last Quarter of the Eighteenth Century*, Liverpool, 1853, p. 177.
[38] *Autobiography and Correspondence of . . . Mrs. Delany*, Second Series, I. 239.
[39] *H. M. C. Egmont*, II. 215, III. 22.

Charles, the Duke of Chandos' valet, became a surgeon.[40] Joseph Bramah, the father of the perfector of the water closet, having been coachman in the Earl of Strafford's family, spent the later years of his life as a tenant on one of His Lordship's estates.[41] Lord Palmerston's coachman also eventually became a tenant of a farm that belonged to his former master.[42] And Mr. Newport, who had been butler to the Duke of Northumberland, became gaoler of New Prison, Clerkenwell.[43]

One occupation stands out as having been especially favoured. A great many domestics became keepers of public houses. They did so, according to Sir John Fielding, because they lacked the training and experience requisite for success in other lines.[44] A more compelling explanation for their preference is that the skills and training required for service were also ideal equipment for tavern keeping. But whatever the reason, there is no doubt that they were to be found operating hostelries of all kinds. Writing in 1777, a newspaper correspondent observes how "The menial servant tired of his Master's *company,* and mid-night revels, becomes the landlord of a snug public house," and how "The *Lady's-Maid,* sick with hasty jaunts and toilet fancies, listens to *Phillip's* soothing tale, then tastes hymenial joys, and takes up her *constant residence* in the bar of a coffee-house. . . ." [45] A review of Patrick Colquhoun's *Observations and Facts Relative to Public-houses* written in 1797 likewise calls attention to the frequency with which servants set up as publicans and innkeepers:

When we consider who are the sort of persons who occupy public houses of every sort, from the best inn on the Bath road to the lowest small-beer pothouse, or hedge ale-house, they are servants of all descriptions; the butler and the housekeeper, the footman and the lady's maid, the coachman and the cook, the gardener and the dairy-maid, the groom, or stable-boy, with the nursery-maid, or kitchen-maid, the carter and the plough-boy with maid-servants of their own rank, whether they have acquired an independent competency by cheating their masters and mistresses, or by long and faithful service, all direct their settlements for life to a public house.[46]

[40] *James Brydges First Duke of Chandos,* p. 174.
[41] Wilkinson, *Worthies, Families and Celebrities of Barnsley,* p. 226.
[42] Tipping, *English Homes,* Period VI. I. 244.
[43] *Lloyd's Evening Post,* 1779, XLV. 419b.
[44] Fielding, *Origin and Effects of a Plan of Police,* p. xi; *London Chronicle,* 1757, II. 221a. Cf. Hanway, *Eight Letters,* p. 60.
[45] *Morning Post,* 1777, No. 442, June 4, 4a. Cf. Daniel Defoe, *The Complete English Tradesman,* 1745, 5th ed., II. 315.
[46] *Gentleman's Magazine,* 1797, LXVII. 223.

These general statements are substantiated by a good deal of other evidence. The King's Head Tavern at Islington was kept in the 1730's by Mrs. Robotham, a former servant of Elizabeth Purefoy.[47] The George Inn at Warminster was taken in 1774 by Simon Hayward, who had been butler to Edward Southwell.[48] The Red Lion Inn at Bagshot was taken in 1780 by Peter Harvey, who had formerly been cook to the Duke of Bolton.[49] The White Swan Inn at Alnwick was occupied in 1782 by a man named Wilson, who at one time had lived as footman in the Hervey family.[50] The Essex Head Tavern in London, the meeting place of the club of that name organized by Dr. Johnson in 1783, was run by Samuel Greaves, a former servant of the Thrales.[51] And the Fountain Inn at Biggleswade was opened in 1790 by J. Scarborough, who had served as butler to the Duke of Chandos.[52]

A career of service often made possible the accumulation of the modest capital necessary to set up in such a business. This is evident from the remarks of an anonymous author who lamented the destiny of retired servants. ". . . they marry," he wrote, "and pine away their small Gains in some petty Shops, or Publick Houses. . . ."[53] The same inference may be drawn from the observations of "Footmanius," who in 1762 addressed himself on the subject of vails to the editor of a London newspaper: ". . . if a servant chances to save a little money in his place why it enables him to get into some business, and keep his family from going to the Parish. . . ."[54]

Service also often provided the domestic with a beneficent patron through whose efforts he gained suitable employment or was launched in a suitable trade. The patron might either be one of his employers or else some person he had met through one of his employers; the patron's efforts might take the form of either financial assistance or the exercise of influence.

A proposal that Thomas Whitehead, while in the service of the

---

[47] *Purefoy Letters,* II. 240.

[48] *London Chronicle,* 1774, XXXVI. 39a.

[49] *London Courant,* 1780, May 20, 4c.

[50] "Journals of the Hon. William Hervey, in North America and Europe, from 1755 to 1814", *Suffolk Green Books,* XIV, 335.

[51] *Letters of Samuel Johnson LL.D.,* ed. G[eorge] B. Hill, Oxford, 1902, II. 390n.

[52] *Torrington Diaries,* II. 276n. For further examples see *ibid.,* I. 352; *Autobiography and Correspondence of . . . Mrs. Delany,* First Series, III. 423; Stirling, *Annals of a Yorkshire House,* II. 311; *Diary of John Baker,* p. 412; *Wynne Diaries,* II. 199; *Memoirs of . . . Mrs. Catherine Cappe,* p. 55.

[53] *An Enquiry into the Melancholy Circumstances of Great Britain,* p. 21.

[54] *London Chronicle,* 1762, XI. 380b.

Duke of Kingston, received from a former master well illustrates how the kind employer might finance a servant. After Whitehead had been valet to the Duke for a number of years, Sir Henry Oxenden, with whom he had previously lived, sent for him and offered to put him in possession of the Crown Inn at Rochester.[55]

One of Whitehead's fellow servants received financial aid from a similar source. Mr. Frozard, who had entered the Duke's employ as a youth and had eventually been advanced to the post of butler, on quitting service took Hall's Stables at Hyde Park Corner. His savings made up part of the necessary funds; but he was also assisted by Col. Litchfield, a former employer, who had recommended him as a boy to the Duke.[56]

Robert Dodsley's retirement from service was also made possible by a generous gift, although in this case the donor had never been his master. The son of a country schoolmaster, Dodsley was early apprenticed to a stockinger; but disliking the work, he ran away and became a domestic. He may have gone up to London to look for a place, or he may have been taken up by some employer who had engaged him in the country. In any case, soon after his arrival there, he entered the household of Charles Dartiquenave, the epicure. It is possible that he next served Sir Richard Howe, who, he said, encouraged him to write verse. The turning point in his career occurred when, about 1728, he became footman to Jane Lowther, daughter of the first Viscount Lonsdale. In her house he came in contact with a host of literary celebrities, some of whom probably took notice of him. Moreover, she is said to have placed her library at his disposal. As a result, his muse thrived. In 1729 he published *Servitude,* after Defoe had revised it and supplied a preface and postscript. A second edition bearing the title *The Footman's Friendly Advice to His Brethren of the Livery* was brought out the next year; and this was followed in 1732 by *A Muse in Livery, or the Footman's Miscellany,* a collection of verse. The eighteenth century's interest in untutored genius rather than the intrinsic merit of these works gave Dodsley something of the vogue enjoyed by Stephen Duck, the thresher-poet, and Anne Yearsley, the poetical milkwoman. Like several other literary domestics, including Mary or Molly Leapor, whose poems first appeared in 1748,[57] and Elizabeth Hands, whose verses were initially published in the news-

---

[55] Whitehead, *Original Anecdotes,* pp. 128–9.
[56] Whitehead, *Original Anecdotes,* p. 187.
[57] *Gentleman's Magazine,* 1784, LIV. 806–7.

papers of Birmingham and Coventry and then reprinted in a collected edition about 1787,[58] Dodsley was hailed as clear proof that poetic spirit might be found in the scullery and the pantry as well as in the library and the study. Successful as a poet, Dodsley next became a playwright, turning out a piece in prose entitled *The Toy-shop*. Through the influence of Pope, whose acquaintance he had probably made at his mistress', if not earlier at Dartiquenave's, *The Toy-shop* was produced in 1735. Soon after it had been put on, Dodsley left service to become a bookseller and publisher. The proceeds of the play, along with his savings, helped to establish him in his new occupation. But a donation of a hundred pounds from his patron, Pope, was perhaps decisive in enabling him to make the change.[59]

The exertion of influence, the other way a patron might render assistance, is exemplified by the manner in which many domestics entered government service. Undoubtedly there were some who, having laid up sufficient funds, purchased comfortable berths. This is evidenced by an advertisement that appeared in 1796:

A Sober Steady Elderly Man, who has passed the principal part of his time in servitude, with reputation and profit to himself, wishes to pass the remainder of his days in some easy situation, in any of the Public Offices, where much attendance or the exertion of literary talents may not be deemed necessary. A handsome gratuity will be given to any Person who can procure the advertiser such a situation.[60]

But the majority of those who entered government service did so through the good offices of their masters. It was a common thing for a master to use his connexions to obtain a post for a deserving servant. In 1750 a writer grumbled that

if any gentleman of a small estate applies to a lord or member of parliament, to get some little place in the government's service for a younger son, he may perhaps succeed, after his lordship or his honour, has provided for all his favourite servants, even down to his postilion; for the footman or valet of a lord, or member, now stands a better chance of being thus provided for, than the best qualified poor gentleman in the kingdom.[61]

[58] W. K. Riland Bedford, *Three Hundred Years of a Family Living*, Birmingham, 1889, pp. 112–13.
[59] Straus, *Robert Dodsley*, pp. 1–37.
[60] *Morning Chronicle*, 1796, No. 8273, Apr. 15, 4a.
[61] *London Magazine*, 1750, XIX. 558.

BIBLIOGRAPHY

M. Dorothy George, *London Life in the 18th Century*, London, 1925.
Dorothy Marshall, *English People in the Eighteenth Century*, London, 1956.
Katharine West, *Chapter of Governesses: A Study of the Governess in English Fiction, 1800–1949*, London, 1949.

"ELITE" AND "NOBILITY" IN THE SECOND HALF OF THE 18TH CENTURY IN FRANCE *

Marcel Reinhard

Changes in the concept and the composition of the elite reveal changes in the type of stratification system. For the case of the French elite from the early eighteenth to the early nineteenth century, Reinhard traces both kinds of change. Even though this period includes the Revolution, conflicting values and social pressures interacted in such a way as to produce modifications of both the concept and the composition of the elite, rather than their radical transformation. From this it may be concluded that the stratification system similarly was modified rather than transformed.

Marcel Reinhard is Professor and Director of the Institute for the Study of the French Revolution at the Sorbonne. Besides having been the Director of a History of France, he has written on Napoleon, Carnot, and Henri IV.

One of the most important aspects of the French Revolution was the profound transformation of the concept of the elite. This transformation produced a split between the concept of elite and that of "nobility." The decline of the nobility benefited the new elite, and ultimately there emerged what was predominantly a society of "capable persons" (*capacités*) instead of an aristocratic society. . . .

---

* Reprinted from Marcel Reinhard, "Elite et noblesse dans la seconde moitié du XVIIIe siècle," *Revue d'histoire moderne et contemporaine*, January–March, 1956. By permission.

Early in the eighteenth century, it was still a common practice to assert that the concepts of "elite" and "nobility" were identical. The nobility comprised persons of quality endowed with hereditary excellence (*vertu*) and talents. LaRocque's classic work, *Traité de la noblesse*, published in 1735, sets forth this thesis clearly. Nobility is identified with excellence, initially that of the ancestors and necessarily that of their descendants. The doctrine is biological. "The seed of procreation possesses some undefined power—some undefined principle—which transmits to the offspring the excellence of their parents." . . .

The nobility, then, was an *"élite de race."* And yet La Rocque did not endow it with a monopoly of virtues, or even of nobleness. He noted the existence of other nobilities whose origin was different: the military nobility, the administrative nobility (*noblesse de charges*), the literary nobility, the spiritual nobility, etc. . . . He confined himself to an enumeration, based on documents, without venturing to comment. Others, long before him, had ventured to do so. So François Patrice, who early in the sixteenth century, had contrasted the aristocrats of birth with "those who by virtue of loftiness and nobleness of spirit have exalted themselves and built upon their virtues." And he did not hesitate to grant the latter preeminence: "These are the true aristocrats." . . .

Two social structures, and two ethics as well, were in opposition. It is indeed true that the scale of values was a shifting one. La Rocque recognized the diversity of merits and their changing prestige.

At first it was military excellence that predominated. For a very long time, from the Feudal Age to that of the Saint-Cyriens in the nineteenth century, it seemed to be the major virtue, that of so-called hereditary and military nobility (*noblesse de race et de l'épée*). But the bravery of the troop commander, the general's quick appraisal of the military situation, and the technical knowledge of the strategist—these were to be found also in men of common origin; while the aristocrat had trouble in adapting himself to the demands of a kind of warfare whose technique was becoming more scientific. Moreover, from Erasmus to the abbé de Saint-Pierre, Rousseau, and Kant, the preeminence of the military virtues was increasingly being challenged. Culture, humanism, and artistic talent were vying with military excellence —as was the learning and skill of legal and financial officials. It is significant that a man like Roederer brought up the complaints made against Francis I for having degraded the old nobility in creating knights of law and of letters. Might he not as easily have blamed the founder of the Order of Saint-Michel? All of society was in fact in-volved—including the economy, which was creating for the wholesale merchants (*négociants*) their well-established importance. . . .

In effect, people no longer adhered to the Pascalian conception of different categories of elites, distinct and juxtaposed, and they no longer accepted the classification of men "by externals, as by nobility or property." The image of the replacement of the vertical lines of feudal society by horizontal courses (layers) of social classes seems appropriate. Would it be possible to ensure the stability of society and of the political system by means of individual preferments—thus re-generating the nobility and appeasing the hostility of the most eminent of the non-nobles? Should one ennoble entire social categories, as had been done in the case of the *robins* (those connected with the law)? It was the responsibility of the monarchy, which alone was qualified to ennoble and which was directly concerned, to decide upon a policy and put it into effect. There was reason to believe that it had done so when, in 1750, it created the military nobility.

The Military Nobility

Although generally accepted, the term "military nobility" is de-plorably ambiguous. It refers neither to an aristocracy which is military (as distinct from other aristocracies), nor to the ennoblement of all officers, but rather to an inchoate kind of nobility, granted under cer-tain conditions of service and seniority. The general intent was a kind of decoration, with or without pecuniary privilege.

The decree tended to recognize the military order as a corporate, professional body; the basis for this recognition lay in the military calling itself. Being an army officer was traditionally considered a career suitable for nobles. The prestige of the sword survived in a society emerged from feudalism. Officers lived nobly in any case; and the nobles who had served along with them in the field could more easily admit them to their own society than they could admit, for example, a bourgeois who had been raised to an administrative position. More-over, military service was also the service of the king; and the fact of having served the king well was valid grounds for ennoblement. It is to be noted, indeed, that the beneficiaries were in the habit of com-paring the requirements they had to meet with those applicable to the men of the robe.

Thus the edict had its roots in the past, both distant and recent.

There is reason to believe, moreover, that it was connected with other policies soon to go into effect: if the claims of the *négociants* were to be recognized, and if commercial as well as administrative functions might thus confer ennoblement, it was inconceivable that military service alone should not.

It is nonetheless remarkable that the edict promulgated on 27 November 1750 was the first extensive measure taken by the monarchy to modify the recruitment of the nobility by a general provision, while ostensibly restoring it to its original state.

The Preamble states:

The most ancient nobility of our realm, which owes its first origin to the glory of arms, will no doubt (*sic*) learn with pleasure that we regard the transmission of its privileges as the most gratifying award that those who have followed its example in war could possibly receive. Already ennobled by their deeds (*sic*), they possess the worth of the nobility even though they do not yet possess the title.

This distinction between nobility of personal merit and legal nobility is significant. . . .

The measure went into effect immediately as regards *roturiers* generals (generals not of noble birth), but it seems that there were only a very few of them at this time. A few others were ennobled after regular promotions, especially at the time of the large-scale promotions of 1780 and 1784. But it is difficult to distinguish the *roturiers* on these lists: at the best estimate there were about 50 such *maréchaux de camp* (out of more than 770) and five or six lieutenant generals (out of about 200).[1]

It would appear that the high aristocracy did not really protest, except for a few scornful remarks like those quoted by the biographers of Chevert.

On the other hand, the ennobling of the company-grade and field-grade officers was on a much larger scale, and the nobility resented it,[2] although a kind of compensation had been granted to impoverished nobles by the establishment of the Military Academy (in that same

[1] See the military registers, and especially the notes of S. Churchill accompanying the re-edition of 1789. Among the commoners promoted to the rank of general were the chiefs of the technical services, Corps of Engineers and Artillery, where skill played a role such that they could be classified among the engineers—together with their colleagues of the Civil Engineering Service, for example.

[2] Barbier on the contrary, enthusiastically approved the edict (*Journal*, t. III, p. 188), as did Voltaire (*Essai sur les moeurs*, édit. Moland, t. II, p. 498).

year of 1750) and by the promise that the venality of commissions would soon be abolished. As early as 1757, the Comte de Gisors wrote to his father, the Maréchal de Belle-Isle, that the edict was prejudicial to *"la pauvre et vraie (sic) noblesse."* [3] And in 1758 Belle-Isle tried to abolish the venality of commissions, and to retire—in the middle of a war—those sub-lieutenants, cornets, and ensigns who could not show a certificate of nobility. It became apparent, however, that the situation was irretrievable: nobles would furnish unsubstantiated certificates as favors to bourgeois who were their creditors or their protégés, or with whom they had family connections. And when, in 1763, Choiseul ruled that *roturiers* should be discharged before the nobles, the same difficulties were encountered.[4] *Roturiers* were found even in the King's Guard. The regulation of 22 December 1758 stipulated that members of the Guard should be chosen from among the noblemen; but the sons of those living nobly were also acceptable.[5] This is why we find numerous letters of nobility conferred on officers of the King's household; for the plain fact is that the nobles were too poor to meet the expenses of the King's service.

For this same reason, the nobles assisted the bourgeois individually.

Colonels auctioned off lieutenant's and captain's commissions; noble officers sold their commissions to commoners; and the sons of wealthy bourgeois were to be found even in the Military Academy.[6] The impecuniosity of the nobles made some of them very obliging vis-à-vis commoners, but this surely served only to embitter the aristocracy as a whole. It was the cause of the famous Edict of 1781, issued just when the third generation of military nobles created by the edict of 1750 was coming along: henceforth there would be very few soldiers of fortune whose rapid promotion opened the door to ennoblement. For that matter, access was being denied on every hand: beginning in 1788, only members of the high nobility were qualified, in principle, for the higher ranks; and the same held true for the King's Guard. This is the classic case of aristocratic reaction. . . .

Regardless of the role of wealth in producing a military nobility, the ennobling of the military hardly modified the old concept of an elite that was based squarely on military virtues. At the very most, the policy of ennoblement took newly into account the importance of

[3] Tuetey, *Les officiers d'ancien régime*, pp. 255ff.
[4] Carré, *La noblesse de France et l'opinion publique au XVIIIe siècle*, p. 161.
[5] Tuetey, *op. cit.*, p. 121.
[6] Tuetey, *op. cit.*, p. 131; Carré, *op. cit.*, p. 160.

length of service. From the point of view of the society, it scarcely altered the traditional structure; most noticeably, it deprived the nobles of positions to which they were so much attached that they went so far as to assert that the Royal Army should have the precise number of officers' berths required to accommodate all the nobles who wanted them. The split between elite and nobility appears, however, in the case of the commercial nobility.

The Commercial Nobility

"So long as Europe was exclusively given over to the military, the sovereigns who had need of soldiers granted distinctions to the military profession. . . . Now that Europe is becoming commercial, the sovereigns need merchants." [7] It was in these terms that, in 1754, Gournay proposed the principle of ennobling of merchants—almost at the same time that the *abbé* Coyer was calling for the orientation of the nobility to commercial activity.[8] The economic boom may very well explain the date of these remarks.

The authorization to conduct wholesale trade had, of course, long since been granted to the nobles; but there has been less emphasis on the ennobling of the wholesale merchants. . . .

The decree of the Council dated 30 October 1767 confirmed the fact that the nobles had been authorized to engage in wholesale trade; but all it granted to the merchants was certain honorary distinctions which brought them closer to the nobility without actually giving them access to that class:

His Majesty desires and ordains that they be considered as living nobly (*vivant noblement*), that they have corresponding rank and seating in municipal assemblies and other such, that they be exempt from service in the militia, and that they wear the sword in the city and bear arms when travelling.

The effect of this was to strengthen the legal status of that intermediate class, alien and inferior to the nobility but placed at the head of the Third Estate—the bourgeoisie who lived nobly. The structure of the French bourgeoisie continually increased the number of steps in its hierarchy without ever breaching the boundary between nobles and

[7] Gournay, Letter dated 10 April 1754 (quoted by Schelle, *Gournay*, p. 69).
[8] Coyer, *La noblesse commerçante*, 1756.

non-nobles. Those physicians, lawyers, and judges who did not have a position conferring nobility, together with those landowners who subsisted on their income alone, belonged to the bourgeoisie that lived nobly, and accordingly received certain privileges. For instance, their children did not run the risk of humiliation by being barred from certain positions, because their "humble extraction" made them unworthy.[9] But this was not an innovation; nor was it a measure calculated to give satisfaction to the merchants. On the contrary, it had the effect of emphasizing the fact that they remained outside the nobility, of identifying them with a class more impatient than any other at not being ennobled.

And yet the decree granted a contemptibly limited concession: the annual promulgation of *two* letters of nobility in favor of important merchants who were the sons and grandsons of distinguished merchants. . . .

So the monarchy vindicated Gournay: nations had need of merchants as well as of military men. But their claims did not rest on the glamour of courage, on devotion to the King, on impressive deeds. These claims were based on social utility rather than on personal merit or on the desirability of granting a reward to those already made wealthy by their success. The number of those who actually benefited was ridiculously small—a fact which seemed to give the lie to the principles so emphatically proclaimed, and to reveal the reluctance with which the Royal Government acknowledged an economic elite. . . .

Moreover, the King did not look with favor on adventurous pioneers. He preferred to reward practical wisdom and foresight, "prudence in undertakings, accuracy in correspondence, good faith in commitments, and punctuality in filling them." This is a veritable eulogy of bourgeois virtues, an attitude fitting for a nation of lawyers, and also a precaution against the possible discredit of a commercial nobility that included merchants in a state of bankruptcy. . . .

All in all, the policy of ennobling merchants was applied in conformity with the strictness of the Edict of 1767. According to the Paris sources, no more than 31 letters were granted between 1767 and 1787. The greatest number—three or four per year—were granted in 1775, 1776, and 1785, which suggests that, for all of France, the total reached 40 letters in these 20 years.[10] . . .

[9] The son of a tanner and innkeeper of Avallon was barred for reasons of low birth when his father tried to purchase for him a position as Crown Prosecutor (Tartat, *Avallon au XVIIIe siècle*, t. II, p. 55). The same was true of admission to the military academies before the decree of 1781.

[10] Du Halgouet, *Les gentilhommes commerçants en Bretagne aux XVIIe et*

Thus it was an attempt that failed. Those who petitioned for letters of nobility were not always well reputed or representative merchants. The latter found it simpler, surer, and quicker to buy an office as secretary to the King, together with a few chateaux and a few estates. . . .

The Aristocracy of Talents

"Even without letters of nobility," wrote Robespierre, "genius is always noble." [11] This was the predominant opinion among enlightened persons in the eighteenth century. It is of some importance to ascertain whether the monarchy took this opinion into account in granting letters of nobility. Such an attitude would have been consistent at least with current norms if not with current practice: it would have proven that the monarchy understood how the concept of the elite had been transformed. . . .

It would have made a significant difference if, in the age of enlightenment, when authors, artists, and engineers were emerging as the elite of the "men of talent," the monarchy had confirmed these views and obtained the support of this elite for the régime. Of course, this would have meant a commitment extending far beyond the mere granting of letters of nobility. [12]

First of all it is to be noted that the spiritual aristocracy—if by that we mean the ecclesiastical—was not represented in the aristocracy of talent. This was the period when bishops of common birth, amiably nicknamed "violet valets (*cuistres violets*), were no longer tolerated in office.

The lawyers, soon to become the leaders of the Constituent Assembly, likewise had hardly any share in the benefits of ennoblement. And yet they constituted a prestigious group that could claim ennoblement by virtue of an old institution that had fallen into disuse—the *noblesse de lettres*. The few lawyers who were ennobled were beholden for the fact to public services they had rendered, or to attainments of a rather special nature; e.g., the case of a certain Grignon, who had discovered a long-buried city near Saint-Dizier. The monarchy could not win

---

XVIIIe siècles, 1936, p. 169. He reports 22 cases of the ennoblement of merchants in Brittany for the entire eighteenth century.

[11] Robespierre, *"Eloge de Gresset,"* Oeuvre, t. I, p. 113.

[12] In France, "authors possess a kind of noble status," wrote the Englishman, John Nickolls: *Remarques sur les avantages et les désavantages de la France et de la Grande Bretagne par rapport au commerce*, 1754. Cf. also F. Menéstrier, *De la Chevalerie ancienne et moderne*, 1683.

the sympathies of so powerful a guild; or rather, it seems not to have suspected its power.

Physicians and surgeons, however, were rather frequently honored with letters of nobility: 31 of them between 1750 and 1785, as against three between 1738 and 1750. It was the continuation of a tradition. . . .

We find, indeed, that the ennobled physicians and surgeons were so often attached to the person of the King and to those around him, that they might very well be placed in the category of *"nobles domestiques"* according to La Rocque's classification. It is true that the physicians in attendance upon the princes were, in principle, supposed to have been chosen from among the most eminent. More often than not, they belonged to various academies, French and foreign. Thus it was fairly logical to confirm those honors and to believe that in this way ennoblement would reward the elite of the medical profession. Were not the academies the meeting-places of the elite, where nobles and men of talent were on equal terms?

Yet not all the members of the Academy of Medicine were ennobled; and other medical men who were merely distinguished practitioners, were ennobled: some for having combated epidemics; others for having provided instruction that would reduce the frequency of "those evils which, in the provinces, affect pregnant women and infants"; and still others for having worked on behalf of inoculation. The history of medicine is still too little known to permit the assertion that those ennobled were actually the best men.

The case of Quesnay raises the question of the ennoblement of the physiocrats and of economists more generally. Quesnay was rewarded, so his letters of nobility state, for "the very distinguished studies he [has] published on the most important aspects of medicine." Is it simply care not to mention Quesnay's articles in the *Encyclopédie* that explains such reticence with respect to his work as the leader of the physiocrat school?

Dupont de Nemours and Abeille did not receive letters of nobility until late—the former in 1783 and the latter in 1787—both in their capacities as inspector-general of commerce. . . . Honors of this kind accrued, in effect, not to the men themselves but to their official functions, like a decoration at the end of a career. Dupont de Nemours had the honor of having the Duc de la Rochefoucault, the Marquis de Mirabeau, and Lavoisier vouch for his attainments at the time of the traditional inquiry.

The savants were not treated any better. One searches through the registers in vain for the names of Monge, Berthollet, Baumé, Bailly, Borda, Lalande, or Laplace. Even the kind of fervent admiration that brought Nollet a large and brilliant audience, did not suffice to earn him ennoblement. The mathematician Le Blond did obtain it, but only because he was instructor to the royal children.

By contrast, applied science was much favored, especially when practiced by engineers belonging to such official bodies as the Corps of Engineers, the Navy, and the Civil Engineering Service (*Ponts et Chaussées*). The construction of roads, levees, ports, and seagoing ships was as much vaunted as military exploits. Among the ten or so persons of this category who were ennobled between 1750 and 1789 was Perronet, founder and director of the Ecole des Ponts et Chaussées.

This modernization of the nobility is also evident in the case of Pierre Morat, ennobled because he had devoted himself "from his earliest youth to the study of mechanics," and because he had organized a fire brigade efficient enough to put out the fire at the Hôtel Dieu. The time was to come when the men of the Revolution would retrieve and make use, almost verbatim, of the King's declaration concerning the rewards due to "those distinguished talents to whom the Nation is indebted for discoveries whose utility is well recognized."

The discrepancy between the distribution of honors and that of abilities appears even more clearly in the field of literature. The *encyclopédistes* were ignored even more completely than the physiocrats. Although adulated by the enlightened despots, these writers were snubbed by their own King. Was it in order to avoid unflattering comparisons that he also snubbed the celebrities of the day—the Barthélemys, the Delilles, the Lebrun-Pindares, and others of the stamp of Suard? The ennobling of Gresset could hardly compensate for these omissions, especially since it was fortuitous. (Gresset had the good luck to have been selected to salute Louis XVI, upon his accession to the throne, in the name of the French Academy.)

So far, our investigation of the recognition of talent by the monarchy has been disappointing. In the arts, there is more evidence of such recognition, even though literary activity had never been considered derogating, whereas artistic creation was exempt from derogation only if it had no commercial character. If artists were now more favored than writers and men of learning, this may, of course, have had something to do with the fact that their art was remote from the new political ideas, which were regarded as subversive.

Among those granted letters of nobility between 1750 and 1785, 25 belonged to the world of the arts. Here the choices were intelligent. They included talented architects like Lassurance, Soufflot, and Mique; excellent painters like Van Loo, Natoire, Lemoine, and Vien; eminent engravers like Roettiers and (especially) Cochin; sculptors like Pigalle and Coustou; and, in music, Rameau. If the King no longer discovered great artists, he at least endorsed them by "bestowing upon the arts and those who practice them with celebrity (sic) distinctive tokens of [his] patronage."[13]

In the end, the "men of talent" did receive 60 letters of nobility between 1750 and 1789—a share that was remarkable and unprecedented, and that committed the monarchy to a policy of expanding the nobility in terms of modern conceptions of the elite. Unfortunately, the import of this innovation was reduced by the uneven distribution of the letters among the different categories of talent, and among the eligible men. . . .

The Nobility of Public Office

The question that must be answered is whether "so-called principles shall no longer yield to the most eminent capability and merit—whether merchants and artists alone are to obtain letters of nobility; as though the title of magistrate was not the first in importance; as though the magistrature no longer needed to be supported by honor and honorable distinctions." Thus Turgot in 1775.[14]

This blast was directed against something that was more of a trend than a reality, because at the time the position of magistrate still led more often to ennoblement than did commerce or the arts. Between 1750 and 1788, at least 100 letters of nobility were granted to magistrates and other public officials; and this figure is based only on Paris sources; nor does it take into account those magistrates ennobled by their

[13] The lists published by Guiffrey (Revue historique, 1873, and Nouvelles archives de l'art français, 1883) make no mention of Van Loo, Lassurance, Natoire, La Guêpière, Mique, Pigalle, Silvestre, Couture (Arch. nat. P 2592, 2597, Bibliothêque nationale, ms. français, 32889); Godet de Soudé, Dictionnaire des Ennoblissements. Caffiéri petitioned for letters of nobility in 1790. (J. J. Guiffrey, Les Caffiéri, p. 388). Up to that time the ennobling of artists had been rather exceptional.

[14] Letter of 28 December to Esmangart, Intendant of Caen; Arch. du Calvados. This letter throws light on Turgot's character and shows that his attachment to those serving the nation was stronger than his esteem for the economists and business men.

particular office—something not so rare as has been supposed, as M. Egret has shown. . . .

Most significant was the ennoblement of officials as such; e.g., of the inspectors-general of commerce, of military engineers who had attained to the higher ranks, of the engineers of the Ponts et Chaussées, or of the head clerks in the ministries. The judiciary was losing its monopoly. Noble status could be attained without buying an office—simply by following a course of study and working in the various important services of the monarchy. In this way the dignity of the modern disciplines—scientific and economic—was endorsed. Unfortunately, the importance of these measures was diminished by their infrequency; nonetheless, a nobility of officials was taking form. The time would come when Napoleon would simply draw the obvious conclusions from these precedents.

Certain usages which led to ennoblement more or less haphazardly were discontinued; and there is reason to believe that this too indicated concern for rewarding real abilities. Thus it had been traditional to ennoble those municipal magistrates who had received the King in their cities when he was making a journey. Shortly after the visit made by Louis XVI in 1786 to Cherbourg and Caen, the officers of those cities attempted to benefit from this usage, and were refused.

Philanthropy, on the other hand, constituted valid grounds for ennoblement.

In a great many cases, acts of charity were adduced: gifts or advances to hospitals on the part of merchants; distribution of foodstuffs during a famine; establishment of shelters for orphans; help to the poor and the sick. Virtue and devotion to the common weal were rewarded by ennoblement. Was it done with discernment? In general, philanthropy was considered to be a supplement to claims that were a bit slim, and sometimes the authorities used a candidate's philanthropy by way of displaying a sensibility more spectacular than substantial. . . .

The Revolutionary Elite

By the end of 40 years the King had ennobled about 400 families, or ten per year—a proportion completely inadequate to form an elite. . . . The timid policy of the monarchy favored the transition from a feudal society to a capitalist society, without making a place in the elite for men of talent.

"Kings can create *anoblis* [persons who have been ennobled] but not nobles," Saint-Simon had said [15] and experience was confirming this disdainful statement. In fact, usage distinguished between the *anobli* and the noble: a son of the former was merely a *gentilhomme;* he was not a person of "condition," or "quality," or "race," or even of "birth." [16] . . .

In sum, the problem of the relations between the elite and the nobility had not been solved. Those who undertook to regenerate the realm had the responsibility for solving this all-important problem.

The solution was preshadowed in the currents of thought, in the projects for reform, in the criticism of the régime. The elite was defined as personal; it was to be characterized by talent, by worth, and by skill in dealing with problems of state. The elite was to be enlightened: it was to be the best part of the Third Estate—the bourgeoisie. Since it was personal qualities that counted, members of the elite might be found in the nobility, in the clergy, and even among the common people; yet in cold fact, since the elite had necessarily to be educated, it was already separate from the commonalty. . . .

The situation might have been clarified by the work of the Constituent Assembly. They accepted "social distinctions based on the common utility" and on talent and worth. The revocation of privileges, and the abolition of the venality of offices, might have opened up the way to a nobility of merit. The King stated that he was prepared to grant letters of nobility for "services rendered to the King and to the Nation." But new and profound difficulties developed.

On the one hand, the nobility in general was already suspect: "an instrument of oppression," as Mirabeau had proclaimed; and this distrust continued to grow. How then could the elite be integrated into such a class?

On the other hand, members of the Third Estate who otherwise differed from one another as much as did Creuzé Latouche and Léonard Bourdon, were concerned for the victory of the bourgeoisie as such. "To allow men of merit and genius, born into the Third Estate, to abandon it and put their intelligence, their talents, and their wealth into the service of another order, is the height of folly and blindness," [17] be-

[15] *Ecrits inédits,* p. 395.

[16] *Dictionnaire historique des moeurs, usages et coutumes des Français,* t. III, p. 178.

[17] Creuzé Latouche, *Mémoires,* p. 41; L. Bourdon, *Motion à l'assemblée du Tiers à Paris,* 7 May 1789. It should be noted that previously these two observers employed the particle in their signatures, thereby indicating a desire to join the *élite nobiliaire.*

cause this would both weaken and degrade the rest of the Third Estate.

Any solution required, as a preliminary step, the abolition of the nobility. Some persons have advanced the opinion that the abolition of feudalism on the night of 4 August, implied the abolition of nobility. Actually, however, when the decree of 15 March 1790 put into effect the decrees of 4 August and 11 August, it was specified only that "all honorary distinctions and superiority of authority resulting from the feudal régime are abolished." [18] Certain jurists—Merlin de Douai, for example—were more concerned with the abolition of the right of primogeniture, made effective by the same decree, "without regard to the previous (*sic*) quality of property or persons." It was not until 19 June 1790 that the abolition of the nobility was accomplished—by a kind of surprise coup, and not without many protests.

Thus the road was clear for an official act of recognition of the elite. Necker had even pointed out that only hereditary nobility had been abolished; and he asked whether personal nobility was being preserved. As a matter of fact, the Assembly was planning to reward the best citizens. On the same day that it abolished the nobility, it granted a badge of honor to the men who had stormed the Bastille: at one blow replacing an order of estates with an order of merit, and taking civic spirit as the criterion of merit.

The new policy was refined and expanded beginning 3 August. "The Nation must reward services rendered to the body social, when their scope and their duration are deserving of this mark of gratitude." This was not the triumph of individualism, as has too often been remarked in every connection, but rather the triumph of the principle of social utility, recently studied by M. Belin. The character of the elite would be determined by the services to be recognized. They were civil and military services; those of artists, scholars, men of letters, and of men who had made "great discoveries of such a kind as to ease the lot of humanity, enlighten mankind, or perfect the useful arts." The Assembly envisioned the selection of such persons even beyond the boundaries of France, projecting a kind of international elite that lacked only the Nobel Prize.

The execution of this policy was upset by the developments of the Revolution, and in particular by egalitarianism. There was, however, a

---

[18] Marquis de Foucault, *Déclaration à l'Assemblée le 19 juin 1790.* Rabaut Saint-Etienne (*Précis de la Révolution,* p. 197) feels the abolition of the nobility should be dated 5 November 1789.

notion that the elections would help to form an elite. Ultimately, the exigencies of the revolutionary struggle were such that civic and patriotic virtues came to be rated more highly than the rest. The elite was composed of the great men, the tribunes, the friends of the people, the victims of the aristocrats—those whose portraits and busts were widely displayed, those who were accorded the honors of the Pantheon. The rewards came either too soon or too late, and generally the glory was ephemeral!

By an unexpected twist, the war alone was to give rise to a large new elite, new even in its structure, though attached to traditions of past military glory. Thus the new nobility was that of the field officers and generals.

It had become imperative, indeed, to adopt again a system of incentives in order to reinforce the patriotism of the military. Although the orders of chivalry had been abolished on 31 July 1791, the Order of Saint-Louis had survived as a military decoration until the fall (in 1792) of the descendant of Saint Louis. Recourse was then had to citations in the Convention, the Order of the Nation, and *armes d'honneur*. To these were added glory, power, and wealth. When the *représentants en mission* disappeared, when the deputies had recourse to the troops, the new elite made a brilliant showing: young, audacious, and sure of itself. This new elite did not become fully visible until after Thermidor.

At the same time the *"nantis"* were declaring that they were the elite of the elect, that property and education were the primary qualifications. They were limiting the franchise, establishing great schools, reviving the academies, and founding the Institute. This take-over was underlined by the revolutionary protest of Babeuf, who loathed both talent and property. In the face of this threat, the new gentlemen began to feel less hostility toward the former nobles. But the military elite was losing patience with the pretensions of the lawyers and all other kinds of "mere civilians." And the members of that elite saw to it that Napoleon triumphed over Sieyès.

The Nobility of the Empire

. . . The imperial nobility marked the culmination of the trend that had begun under the Old Régime in favor of a nobility of officials and a military nobility. In his speech to the Senate, Cambacérès took a dim view of the necessity of recognizing an elite but, rather, stressed the necessity for a monarch to draw strength from hereditary distinctions and thus to fill in a "gap in political organization."

This nobility was administrative. The first titles were awarded to 112 senators, 30 councillors of state, the chairman of the legislative body, and to the archbishops, who became counts; to the presidents of the electoral colleges, to the first presiding judges of the law courts, to the bishops, and to the mayors of the "good cities," who became barons. Also the army again got the lion's share: from the very first days of the Empire, large batches of generals and field officers were made counts or barons. Members of the Legion of Honor could become "chevaliers d'empire," the title being hereditary if they established an entailed estate. . . .

Actually, the army secured for itself more than half of the letters of nobility. The nobility of the Empire was at the outset a military nobility, in accordance with the logic of events under this régime. The functionaries and administrators received more than one-fifth of the letters, as is natural in a régime both authoritarian and administrative. Private individuals, wealthy and/or influential notables, received six per cent of the letters, while the clergy received three per cent. The scholars, physicians, and members of the Institute formed only a tiny group, with about 1.5 per cent of the letters. Finally, the commercial nobility remained in an embryonic state, and the number of ennobled merchants was negligible.

The great advantage possessed by the nobility of the Empire was that it was well enough provided for to keep up a prestigious style of living; and the institution of the entailed estate guaranteed that inheritance would not mean impoverishment.

But the old nobility persisted despite legal measures. Its members were glad to call themselves *ci-devant* marquis or *ci-devant* counts; and the régime came in time to recognize the old nobility—unofficially, at least—when it wanted to make use of the authority of their family connections or their wealth.[19] In time it may have merged with the new nobility; or rather it may have absorbed it, so ruining the efforts that had been made to create a new elite.

Conclusion

By the end of that half-century, marked by so many vicissitudes

---

[19] Confidential circular of 9 April 1813. Mlle. Denise Marais has made a statistical study of the nobility of the Empire, which has not yet been published.

and so much violence, the question of the elite still had not been decided. It might have seemed that the *noblesse de race*—that nobility
linked to landed estates and made up of seigneurs who wore the sword
as evidence of their rank—had been eliminated. But this was not at all
the case.

The Revolution was sometimes too timid, at other times too bold,
and always too unstable, to wipe out age-old social habits. The *noblesse
de race* had lost estates and manors, privileges and functions; it had
seen its wealth seriously depleted, and its most prominent members
take flight, go to prison, or go to the scaffold. But it had managed to
obtain help from devoted friends to save lives and property; it had taken
advantage of periods of calm to recover its strength; and Napoleon himself had offered the old nobility the opportunity to rejoin the Establishment—sometimes even seeming to solicit this action on their part. He
had appreciated the old nobility when looking for young officers, or for
desirable matches in order to carry out a policy of advantageous marriages. The exhaustion caused by the war, and the irritation provoked by
the parvenus who flaunted their epaulettes, militated in favor of re-
examining a case that had once appeared hopelessly lost. The *noblesse
de race* still have its prestige and its opportunities. It had only to make
skillful use of them in order to become, once again, the breeding ground
of the elite.

The commercial nobility, on the other hand, was still-born. It had
been promised a brilliant future by the monarchy; but the deeds of the
monarchy had not been on the same high level as their ideas. Its timid
policy had disappointed the potential beneficiaries without reassuring
their enemies. And yet this preferment would seem to have been required by the new society—a commercial and economic society, dedi-
cated to business. This new elite had come into ever closer contact with
the old nobility by virtue of its style of living, its education, and its
mores. Sedaine, like so many of his contemporaries, had believed this
harmonization would take place. The monarchy had missed an opportunity—one of the last—to adapt the régime to the new era, and to secure
its future.

At the outset, the Revolution was the work of lawyers: despite
repeated efforts, the business interests had no deputies. Being lawyers
and men of property, the members of the Constituent Assembly had
little thought of giving to commerce what they were taking away from
"feudalism." The democratic thrust (for that is what it was) had
attacked the business men as profiteers, exploiters, and reactionaries.

At times when neither speculation nor the procurement of war materiel was important, the groups in power had succeeded one another
without any great advantages to the business men, who no longer even
had the expedient of purchasing offices—as they had previously done
to obtain nobility. Napoleon had little love for manufacturers and
merchants; the few ostentatious gestures he made in their direction did
not deceive anyone. The nobility of the Empire was not commercial.
The elite of commerce was not integrated into the official elite; and it
had but little prestige even in the opinion of the general public. Even
under Louis XV and Louis XVI the prestige of the merchants and
manufacturers was not so diametrically different from that accorded
them by a Paul de Rousiers—who identified the elite with those respon-
sible for "the management of work"—as it was under the Empire. It
was not until the time of Napoleon III that this situation changed,
thus expressing one of the facets of French history: the distrust of
private enterprise, risk, and capitalism; a France of lawyers, not of the
captains of industry.

The "talents" were in the opposition at the end of the Old Régime,
and they still belonged to it under Napoleon. The thinkers, the writers,
the orators had experienced some exciting years during the Revolution;
but the democrats stigmatized the aristocracy of talent as it did those
of birth or of wealth. The Directory offered a respite, to be sure; but
the victorious general soon learned to mistrust the ideologues. . . .

The other skills were scarcely valued at all except in so far as they
aided either the war, which required men of learning, or those successive régimes that solicited the services of those who might make them
appear illustrious. . . .

Even the physicians, who had been traditionally well represented
in the official elite, had retained only a small place—and that under
the proviso that they would devote their skill to the master of Europe
and the great army commanders.

The new elite wore the saber instead of the sword and a resplendent
uniform instead of court dress: it was an elite of the heroes and beneficiaries of the wars. The army that had saved the Revolution had also
forfeited it. The generals had at first defended, then extended, the
national boundaries. They had at first protected, then expelled, the
deputies. They had become marshals, princes, and dukes. They wore
their titles as trophies. Unpolished and given to vulgar display, they
would recognize no quality in the *"pékins,"* as they contemptuously
called the civilians. It was an astonishing kind of nobility, without

counterpart elsewhere in Europe, and without precedent in the recent past. Its emergence and advent to power had been neither desired nor foreseen. How much time would have been required to consolidate it? To sway public opinion in its favor? How many generations would have been required to soften its manners and morals, cultivate its intelligence, and refine its sensibility? The requisite period of time was not to be. Defeat discredited it for a half-century. The toga and landed property fought over the place it vacated.

Only one elite had improved its status: that of the public officials. As far back as the Old Régime it had begun to grow vigorously. Turgot had granted it a real preeminence; and the successive changes of government had often served its cause—so much so that it was the only elite still honored and in its place.

The Revolution had undoubtedly destroyed the *noblesse de robe*: this was in fact the only example of total and final destruction. But some administrators had managed to stand up to the deputies, and had survived them. They alone had managed to occupy a prominent place, after the military, in the nobility of the Empire and in the higher echelons of the Legion of Honor. Quite a few deputies had even reestablished themselves by becoming administrators. For that matter, was not deputyship a kind of administrative function under Napoleon? The higher civil service was beginning to play the impressive role that it has played up to the present time, attracting talents, wealth, and ambitions.

Lacking the factor of heredity, it often compensated therefor by creating dynasties. Its existence clearly demonstrated the strengthening of the state that was even more pronounced in France than elsewhere on the continent. Through the intermediary stage (theatrical and brief) of the marshals and the generals, France had moved from an *élite de race* to an *élite de fonction*, whereas the original hope had been to give it an elite of thought, of commerce, and of virtues. It was the French way of becoming bourgeois.

BIBLIOGRAPHY

Alfred Cobban, *The Social Interpretation of the French Revolution*, Cambridge (England), 1964.

A. Daumard, "Une Référence Pour L'Étude Des Sociétés Urbaines En France Aux XVIIIe Et XIXe Siècles: Projet de Code Socio-Professionel," *Revue d'Histoire Moderne et Contemporaine*, X (1963), 185–210.

Suzanne Keller, *Beyond the Ruling Class: Strategic Elites in Modern Society*, New York, 1963.

M. Kolabinska, *La circulation des élites en France*, Lausanne, 1912.

R. R. Palmer, *Twelve Who Ruled*, Princeton, 1941.

THE REVOLUTIONARY AND NAPOLEONIC ERA: HOW MUCH OF A WATERSHED? *

Franklin L. Ford

Because the problem is so difficult, many historians have simply not tried to answer the question, when did the basic type of European stratification system change from a closed-class or "caste" type to an open-class type of system? Ford has asked and answered this question very briefly in this excerpt from a short essay, and although the answer must be extended and refined, the question is one that every historical account of the eighteenth and nineteenth centuries in European history needs to ask itself. Otherwise, a basic dimension for understanding that history remains obscure.

Franklin L. Ford, Professor of History and Dean of the Faculty of Arts and Sciences at Harvard, has written about both French and German history in the eighteenth century. His two major works are Robe & Sword *and* Strasbourg in Transition.

. . . Let me now state my own conviction that nowhere—neither in administrative innovations, nor in the altered conditions of war, nor in the first uneven surge toward political democracy, nor in the highly charged cultural atmosphere—do we perceive at its clearest the fundamental shift that makes the last years of the eighteenth century and the first of the nineteenth a historical watershed too imposing to be disregarded. The most important change of all occurred in social structure and, equally important, in the way men conceived of social structure. We need above all to consider what it meant for European society to lose the appearance of a hierarchy of legally defined orders of men.

* Reprinted from the article of the same title, *American Historical Review*, LXIX (1963), 18–29.

By the same token, we must consider what it meant to have nakedly revealed the social subdivisions identified by Max Weber in a famous and by no means outdated essay: classes, as economic groupings; status groups, reflecting degrees of honorific recognition; and parties, organized around shared political aspirations, if not always ideals or principles.[1]

It is worth noting in this connection that before 1789 social and political commentators labored under a double handicap in seeking to analyze the realities confronting them. In the first place, the cherished medieval vision of orders—noblemen, clergymen, burghers, peasants—seemed less and less meaningful, even when applied to Europeans who quite clearly, in a technical sense, did belong to nobility or clergy, bourgeoisie or peasantry. What real use, one might ask, was a category that covered English dukes, French lawyers, and the *glota*, the "barefoot gentry" of Poland, or Italian cardinals, Spanish friars, and poor German schoolmasters in clerical garb? What was the bourgeois brotherhood that united town patricians with the poor cobbler who stared hopefully at their shoes? What good did it do to call "peasants" both the independent *laboureur* on his French farm and the miserable worker on a Bohemian estate?

A second, still more serious trouble with the language of corps and orders was that it did not apply at all to large numbers of people who nonetheless deserved to be taken very seriously. The new Manchester textile manufacturer, the Genevan watch exporter only lately arrived from Basel or Lausanne, the immigrant Dutch wine merchant in Bordeaux were not legally "bourgeois" of their cities, but they most assuredly were businessmen. And what of the growing army of workers not accommodated by the guild system—to what order did they belong?

Let us not oversimplify. If it would be wrong to assume that European society before 1789 was in fact a tightly knit system of orders, it would be just as great an error to suppose that classes, status groups, and parties were as yet completely invisible. Quite the reverse was true, as we realize when we read bitter strictures concerning "the rich"—English nabobs back from India, French tax contractors, German speculators in grains. There was an old awareness too of "the poor" as a polyglot, urban-rural mass, an awareness born of countless seventeenth-century upheavals and of eighteenth-century troubles as recent as E. I. Pugachev's vast rebellion in Russia. If there were emergent classes, there were also eighteenth-century social elements whose honorific

---

[1] "Class, Status, Party," *From Max Weber: Essays in Sociology,* tr. and ed. H. H. Gerth and C. Wright Mills (New York, 1946), 180–95.

status escaped the traditional definition in terms of orders. We need
here mention only the place occupied in most countries by the higher
civil service, the major bureaucrats, often humbly born and only mod-
erately wealthy, whose power nevertheless excited both respect and
animosity. And political parties, as Palmer has shown,[2] can be identified
with relative ease by the 1780's: "Patriots" and "Orangists" in the
United Provinces, "Vonckists" and the "Estates Party" in the Austrian
Netherlands, "Republicans," "Moderates," and "Patriots" in beleaguered
Poland.

Yet the language of orders hung on until the Great Revolution, and
in so far as that language expressed the accepted, the respectable way
of describing human relationships, it was itself a conditioning factor
in the situation. For while Europe's population was not, in fact had
never been, neatly subdivided into nobility, clergy, bourgeoisie, peasantry, and certain less general orders, a conventional terminology suggesting that those were the only meaningful rubrics still helped to
shape men's reactions to developments. Edmund Burke, like Montes-
quieu before him, both pleaded for reform and denounced revolution
in the name of healthy relations among stable ranks of men. Gaspar
Melchor de Jovellanos, gifted and enlightened though he was, saw fit
to dramatize Spain's ills in 1787 by composing a poem on the sad
decline of the ancient nobility.[3] In Württemberg and in other German
states, the critics of princely absolutism scarcely went beyond a reasser-
tion of the rights of the legal orders, the *Stände*.[4] Even in the early
polemical writings of the French Revolution, notably including those
of the Abbé Sieyès, we perceive the hold that old terms and categories
had maintained on the political imagination of the day. The confused
vehemence of the 1780's, the impression of issues badly joined, not only
in France but in other countries as well, seems to me to testify to the
inadequacy of an inherited conceptual scheme when applied to recalcitrant circumstances.

It was the pitiless test of power imposed upon most of Europe by
the revolutionary-Napoleonic crisis that killed the old image of society
—not completely nor all at once, to be sure. Vestiges of archaic language
and values have survived to the present day, sometimes twisted to more

---

[2] Palmer, *Age of the Democratic Revolution*, Chaps. XI and XIII.

[3] *La satire de Jovellanos*, ed. Alfred Morel-Fatio (Bordeaux, 1899); cited by
Richard Herr, "The Twentieth Century Spaniard Views the Spanish Enlightenment," *Hispania*, XLV (No. 2, 1962), 185.

[4] F. L. Carsten, *Princes and Parliaments in Germany from the Fifteenth to
the Eighteenth Century* (Oxford, Eng., 1959).

modern polemical uses. (Incidentally, when we label "bourgeois" a sub-urban ranch house, with a television antenna above and a two-car garage on the side, do we speak with the scorn of noblemen, the pride of burghers, the envy of peasants, or the righteous wrath of prole-tarians?) In any case, the false symmetry of a single hierarchy of orders never recovered from the shock it received in the quarter century that opened in 1789.

That the Revolution contained elements of class conflict, in its most precise, economic sense, was apparent even before the Estates-General came together at Versailles. The *Affaire Reveillon* of April 1789, for instance, was a bloody riot touched off by the efforts of two wealthy Parisian manufacturers (members of the Third Estate) to impose lower wage scales. It is my own belief that Marxist historians, from Albert Mathiez to Albert Soboul,[5] have sought to make class conflict explain more facets of the French Revolution than it can in fact account for. It would be foolish, however, to deny that the struggle between poor men and those more comfortable runs back and forth through the historical fabric of the period, from the Faubourg Saint-Antoine to German cities on the Rhine, from the streets of Amsterdam to the shim-mering water front of Naples.

At the same time, we also encounter intensified party strife, the competition of political groups for power as an end in itself. The suc-cession of such groups in the French assemblies—Feuillants, Girondists, *Montagnards, Hébertistes*—is so familiar that it can easily be under-rated as a new chapter in parliamentary history. No less significant, however, was the effect of events in France on other countries, the tendency in one government after another for "anti-" and "pro-French" parties to appear under such conditions as the local situation offered. In England, for example, war fever and the dread of Jacobin excesses combined to discredit Charles James Fox in the 1790's, but not before his collision with Pitt had given a new sharpness to the struggle be-tween Whigs and Tories.

Gradations of social status, no less than economic and political alignments, were deeply affected by the upheaval. In France, and in other lands that experienced even a forced transplantation of the Revo-lution, a decadelong assault both on ecclesiastical independence and on the privileges of birth left the honorific position of clergy and

[5] See esp. Albert Soboul, "Classes and Class Conflicts during the French Revolution," *Science and Society*, XVII (No. 3, 1953), 238–57, and *Les Sans-culottes parisiens en l'an II* (Paris, 1958).

nobility—not to mention their physical base of power, especially in land —damaged beyond hope of complete repair. Admittedly, neither order was destroyed, but henceforth neither could look down with secure disdain on the rest of society. The revolutionaries' glorification of "citizen" as the proudest of all titles, like their insistence that love of country outweighed humble birth, struck at the very roots of inherited rank and at the mystical awe surrounding prelates.

In place of the old determinants of status, certain others gained a degree of general acceptance that they have commanded ever since. I refer to wealth, special abilities, and service to the community (especially if recognized by the bestowal of public office or military rank). Questions might still be asked about an individual's family tree and his way of life, but they seemed less and less relevant when compared with other, more urgent queries: Is he rich or poor? What can he do? What is his present position? The modern status system may seem no more attractive than that of the *ancien régime,* but the differences between the two are unmistakable.

The Imperial Nobility established by Napoleon in 1808 provides, somewhat surprisingly, an excellent example of basic change. To a superficial observer it might appear that the Emperor was simply resurrecting aristocratic privilege, as underpinning for his dynasty. But let us not overlook two features of this new hierarchy. First, its titles were assigned on the basis of military services rendered or public offices already held by the recipients. Ministers and senators became counts; presidents of departmental electoral colleges, higher judges, mayors of the larger cities became barons; members of the Legion of Honor became chevaliers. Second, such a title, even after having been conferred on an individual, could pass to his descendants only if accompanied by a fortune sufficient to support it. To meet this requirement, a prince of the Empire would have to bequeath an estate yielding at least 200,000 francs per year, while the corresponding figure for a count was 30,000, for a baron 15,000, and for a chevalier 3,000.[6] Napoleon visualized not only a nobility of service, but also one that would remain an "upper class" in specifically economic terms. In his shrewd, cynical mind and in the minds of many of his contemporaries there remained no room for arguments about the virtues of aristocratic birth or leisured refinement or genteel poverty.

I have asked for due consideration of a series of institutional, mili-

---

[6] Félix Ponteil, *Napoléon Ier et l'organisation autoritaire de la France* (Paris, 1956), 124.

tary, political, and aesthetic changes and, in slightly more detail, a set of complex but crucial changes in social structure. Any one of these factors might in itself be dismissed as unrepresentative, or at most a matter only of degree. Taken together, however, they reveal a revolution in the fullest sense, a fundamental departure from some of the most important conditions of human life before 1789. The magnitude and the nature of this phenomenon will surely escape the historian whose gaze is riveted on just on country or on only one type of evidence, be it diplomatic correspondence, official enactments, personal reminiscences, or belles-lettres. But the historian who is willing to look up, however briefly, from his specialized labors and to indulge in a panoramic view can scarcely avoid the impression of looking back toward a massive divide, a true watershed.

BIBLIOGRAPHY

Crane Brinton, *The Anatomy of Revolution*, rev. ed., New York, 1952.
———, *A Decade of Revolution, 1789–1799*, New York, 1934.
Elie Halevy, *England in 1815*, trans. by E. I. Watkin and D. A. Barker, rev. ed., London, 1949.

THE BUSINESS INTERESTS OF THE GENTRY IN THE PARLIAMENT OF 1841–47 *

William O. Aydelotte

When the occupations that members of an upper class customarily pursue offer them a diminishing opportunity-structure, some of them can maintain their high position only by moving, or by having their sons move, into relatively new or growing occupations that also rank high. Some members of the landed gentry and nobility of England, we have seen in some previous essays, have for many centuries been moving from the management of land into various political, religious, and commercial roles of high standing, while, for a different set of reasons, move-

* Reprinted by permission of the publishers from the Appendix to G. Kitson Clark, *The Making of Victorian England*, Cambridge: Harvard University Press, Copyright 1962, by G. Kitson Clark. Published in England by Methuen & Co. Ltd. Originally produced as an answer to a question by Dr. Kitson Clark.

*ment was also going on in the opposite direction as well. The unusual
quantitative study by Aydelotte of the overlapping between landed
society and business society shows the significant extent of mobility of
this kind in the governing elite of the mid-nineteenth century.*

*William O. Aydelotte is Professor of History at the University of
Iowa. A specialist in the history of nineteenth century England, he is
a pioneer in the use of new quantitative and scaling methods recently
developed in the social sciences.*

It has never been settled how far the landed gentry in the mid-
nineteenth century were or were not involved in the world of business,
despite the obvious importance of this question for the political history
of the period. It is well known that some landowners did have active
business careers or incidental business interests, but what matters is
how many or how large a proportion did and what is the general tendency of the evidence. I have some information on the gentry who sat
in the Parliament of 1841–47 which may shed light on this subject.
Though these were perhaps not a representative sample of the gentry,
they were at least a politically important section of them, and hence
an appropriate group to examine in considering the political rôle of
that class.

It would be helpful if this question could be studied in the light
of a detailed examination of estate papers, such as Professor David
Spring has made for some of the families of the nobility. Unfortunately
I do not have this kind of information. The large numbers of the group
with which I am dealing make so detailed a survey out of the question.
I do, however, have a good deal of information of another kind: the
business activities and business connexions of these men as reported
in Dod's *Parliamentary Companion,* biographies, handbooks of various
sorts, minutes of the meetings of railway directors, company prospec-
tuses, and a great variety of other sources. This information amounts
altogether to a good deal of material, ample enough so that most points
established by it can be confirmed several times. The picture it presents
is, at least in its general outlines, reasonably clear.

The extent of the business interests of the gentry cannot be established simply by ascertaining the figures and reciting them: there are
some difficult problems of interpretation. Neither the term 'gentry' nor
the term 'business' has a precise meaning, and the results will depend
on the significance assigned to these two words, on how inclusive we
make them. I doubt that any firm definition of either can be devised

which, on the one hand, will be acknowledged by all as conforming to accepted usage and, on the other hand, will be sufficiently detailed and precise to cover all cases. However, it is still possible to follow some rough rules on a common-sense basis.

In regard to businessmen, the principal danger is that of making this category too inclusive and too uncritical. To describe as businessmen all individuals with business connexions of any kind, no matter how minor or incidental, will, I believe, produce an exaggerated picture of the extent of the representation of commercial interests in Parliament. It seems more useful to count as businessmen only individuals engaged in undertakings that would presumably demand a substantial amount of their time: merchants, manufacturers, brewers and distillers, partners in private banks, and merchant bankers. I have not included among the businessmen, unless they were exceptionally active in commercial affairs, East India and West India proprietors or directors of joint-stock banks, of insurance companies or of railways. I have also excluded silent partners, as well as men who owned business properties but did not manage them or who drew income from business enterprises in which they did not take an active part. In other words, I have sought to make a rough distinction between a major and a minor business involvement. My contention is that the number of businessmen among the gentry was, though significant, not large while the proportion of those involved incidentally in business was, on the other hand, very considerable.

It is still harder to work out a rule of thumb for identifying the landed gentry. What general guide should one follow? Should the sons be included, or only the heads of families? Do the baronets belong in the gentry? (Sir Lewis Namier has told me that he would include them.) What about men more distantly related to the gentry, or for that matter to the baronetage and peerage, grandsons and great-grandsons, for example, or those connected only by marriage?

An abstract discussion of these questions seems unlikely to lead to fruitful results. The solution of them depends in part on the nuances of contemporary usage, which are difficult to recapture after the lapse of a century and which, for all we know, may not even have been consistent at the time. To avoid an unprofitable argument I have simply taken an empirical approach and given, in the tables, separate figures for various groups. As a starting-point I have used the second edition of Burke's *Landed Gentry,* the one most nearly contemporary to this Parliament. This is not wholly satisfactory, for Burke does not adequately explain his basis of selection, and I have every reason to believe, after much use of the work, that it was compiled with something less than meticulous care. Yet an attempt to produce a more refined criterion would lead to ambiguities and would probably be useless since the gentry cannot in any case be defined precisely.

In the tables, the figures for the 'gentry' include only men listed in Burke's second edition. Of the 815 men who sat in this Parliament throughout its length I found 234 in Burke, of whom 166 appeared as heads of families, 35 as eldest sons of fathers still living, and 33 as younger sons of fathers living or dead. I found 129 men related to the baronetage: 81 baronets, 22 eldest sons, and 26 younger sons. Figures for the gentry and baronetage, broken down into heads of families and sons, appear in the tables above the horizontal line; they have been thrown together in the figures immediately below the horizontal line.

To provide a basis for comparison I have added to the tables three other groups: (1) the 180 close relatives of peers (8 Irish peers and 172 sons of peers, including sons of Irish and Scottish ones); (2) 115 men more distantly related by descent to the peerage, baronetage and gentry, or related only by marriage; (3) 157 men who so far as I have yet discovered were not related to the peerage, baronetage or gentry at all. These three groups, together with the gentry and baronetage, make up the whole of the membership of Parliament.

The advantage of presenting separate figures for these several groups is that this procedure makes no assumptions as to which ones belong together. By keeping them distinct, it permits the differences between them to appear. The disadvantage is that such small figures are undesirable for statistical purposes, since they are likely to produce freak errors. The larger the figures, the more confidence we can have in the conclusions we derive from them. It would therefore be helpful to coalesce some of these categories, to make them fewer and larger, if this can be shown to be justified. Figures for the gentry and the baronetage were close enough in most cases to make it seem legitimate to put them together, and I have done this in Tables I–V. Table VI, which summarizes part of the information in Tables I–V, shows comparative figures for the gentry according to the narrowest and according to the broadest definition. The percentages are very close. In other words, while there are many different ways of combining this information, it does not in practice seem to matter much which alternative we choose. The general results are much the same, and the heavy involvement of the landed class in business stands out clearly enough no matter how the figures are arranged.

1. Of the 166 heads of families in the landed gentry I find about one-sixth who can be described as businessmen. This is a total of 26 men, or 16 per cent., the first figure in Table I. The group included 10 partners in private banks, 8 merchants, 6 manufacturers, a merchant banker, and an eminent railway chairman.

The railway man was William Ormsby Gore, and the merchant banker William Brown. The 6 manufacturers included 3 in textiles, Peter Ainsworth, William Feilden and Edward Strutt, 2 ironmasters, Joseph Bailey and Richard Blakemore, and the copper-smelter John Henry Vivian, a brother of the first Lord Vivian. The merchants were: William Astell, Daniel Callaghan, Thomas Gisborne, James Matheson, James Oswald, George Palmer, Thomas Sheppard and Robert Wallace. The private bankers were: William Baillie, Reginald James Blewitt, William Joseph Denison, William Evans, John Scandrett Harford, Kedgwin Hoskins, John Pemberton Plumptre, William Morris Read, Edward Royd Rice and Charles Gray Round.

There might be some question about one or two of these. Thomas Gisborne is better known as a landowner; yet his mercantile interests are confirmed by several sources. It is not clear how closely Edward Strutt was connected with the family business; yet he put himself down in Dod as a cotton manufacturer, and he seems to have been identified in the public mind, notably at the time when he received his peerage in 1856, with the manufacturing interest. On the whole the list seems to me fairly reliable.

None of the eldest sons of the gentry were businessmen. Six of the 33 younger sons were, 18 per cent., a proportion close to that for the heads of families. Three of these men were private bankers, Raikes Currie, William Tyringham Praed and Richard Spooner; and three were merchants, David Barclay, Henry Broadley and Aaron Chapman.

The figures for the baronets were very close to these: 12 per cent. of the heads of families and 27 per cent. of the younger sons were businessmen. Only one heir to a baronetcy was a businessman, James Power, a distiller in Dublin. His father was also a distiller in Dublin and received his baronetcy only in 1841.

It must be admitted that on close inspection some of these baronets do not look like very authentic members of the landed class. Of the 10 baronets I have classed as businessmen, 7 were first baronets, of whom

1 obtained his title in 1837, 2 in 1838, and the remaining 4 only in 1841. These first baronets were: Sir William Clay, who had been a merchant and shipowner in partnership with his father; Sir John Easthope, who had been a stock-broker; Sir Josiah John Guest, the ironmaster; Sir George Larpent, a partner in the mercantile house of Cockerell & Co.; Sir John McTaggart, a merchant in London; Sir David Roche, a merchant in Limerick; and Sir Matthew Wood, the hop merchant and former Lord Mayor of London. Two more were only second baronets: Sir John Rae Reid, a partner in Reid, Irving & Co., whose father had also been a merchant; and Sir George Thomas Staunton, the Oriental scholar, who had been active in the East India Company and whose father had business interests in the West Indies. Only 1 of the 10 seems to have had any antiquity of descent, Sir Alexander Cray Grant, the West India planter, who was an 8th baronet, and whose title had been created in 1688.

The sons of baronets in business, also, seem to derive from families recently established and not necessarily connected with the land. James Power, an eldest son, was, as mentioned, the son of a distiller in Dublin who had received his title only in 1841. Of the 7 younger sons who were businessmen, 4 were sons of first baronets: William Beckett, a banker at Leeds; his brother Edmund Beckett Denison, the chairman of the Great Northern Railway; Henry William Hobhouse, a banker at Bath; and Charles Russell, the chairman of the Great Western Railway. Thomas Baring, the leading partner in Baring Brothers, was the younger son of a second baronet. Humphrey St John Mildmay, the fifth son of a third baronet, married into the Baring family and was a partner in the firm from 1823 to 1847. Patrick Maxwell Stewart, a merchant interested in the West Indies, was the son of a fifth baronet whose title dated from 1667, and was brother-in-law of the Duke of Somerset. Of these, perhaps only Mildmay, Stewart and Russell came from families which belonged in any meaningful sense to the landed class.

Clearly the baronetage was a mixed group. Baronetcies were apparently conferred not only on landed families but also on mercantile families which had little connexion with the land. It might, then, seem mistaken to count the baronets with the gentry. Perhaps they should rather be divided into two sections, a landed and a mercantile one. Yet, if the baronets were a mixed group, the gentry were also. It is necessary to distinguish between the contemporary *mystique* or folklore about the gentry and what seem to be the facts. Sir James Lawrence in his *On the Nobility of the British Gentry,* the fourth edition of which appeared in 1840, has a good deal to say about the prescriptive recognition and prestige of the gentry, which baronets or even peers did not necessarily share. The descendants of yeomen, he asserts, can never be gentlemen, though they may make very respectable lords: gentlemen must belong to families whose ancestors have always borne arms. Such a view bears little relation, if we may judge from Burke, to what was accepted as a working guide in practice. The extravagances of Lawrence must be balanced against the methods apparently used by Burke in compiling his reference work, and I incline to give the preference to Burke. In his volumes there appear a substantial number of families of commerical background and obviously recent descent. Indeed, the number of these may actually be larger than it seems on the surface, since genealogies might be exaggerated or distorted, and coats of arms were notoriously falsified. The prefaces to the later editions of Burke are full of apologies for the genealogical absurdities of the earlier editions. The prefaces to the fifth edition (1871) and to the ninth edition (1898) disclaim responsibility for the heraldic bearings cited in the text.

I conclude that the evidence does not warrant the arbitrary exclusion of the baronets, or any section of them, from the landed class. Both the gentry and the baronetage were rapidly recruiting new members from the commercial and professional classes and, in comparing two orders of society, it seems incorrect to exclude recent arrivals in one case while including them in the other. The extensive degree of coincidence in the figures for the baronetage and the gentry is perhaps an additional reason for thinking of them together. What does appear to be true is that in both the baronetage and the gentry the businessmen were usually, though by no means always, either younger sons or recent arrivals.

2. The business connexions of the landed class were, however, far more extensive than the figures in Table I reveal. Many of the gentry, and many also related to the baronetage and peerage, who were clearly not businessmen had, nevertheless, important connexions with the business world. The 166 heads of families in the gentry included 29 railway directors, 21 insurance directors, 9 directors of joint-stock banks, 2 East India proprietors, 3 West India proprietors, 4 interested in coal-mining, 3 in other types of mining in England, 4 involved in docks, 3 in canals, and so forth. Adding together the businessmen and those with minor

business interests of this kind produces a total of 70, or 42 per cent., who were connected with business in one way or another. This information is set forth, for the gentry and the other groups, in Table II.

Perhaps the figures in Table II are the crucial ones for your purpose, since you are interested not merely in the gentry who were businessmen but also in the business associations of those who were principally oriented towards the land. I cannot say how far these connexions involved a subsidiary income from a non-agricultural source. Yet it seems not improbable that they frequently did. A director of a railway, for example, would be likely to have shares in it. Even if he did not, the mere fact that he was a director constituted a significant connexion with the business world.

The figures in Table II are rather high. Yet they are probably an underestimate, and do not tell the whole story. I have excluded a good deal of information that I found, when it did not seem reliably confirmed. Doubtless there was further information that I failed to get and possibly there were other business connexions of this kind, no evidence for which now survives. Also, these figures include only formal business associations, and not investments. Though the field for investment was restricted in these days before the extensive use of joint-stock financing, it was still possible to put money into railways, insurance companies, Government securities, mortgages and urban real estate. If I had the story on all this, the picture might be still more impressive. I did at one time go through the trouble of compiling the information in the two lists of railway investors published in the 1840s. However, I was informed by those who knew more about railway history than I did that these lists were unreliable, and I finally decided not to use them.

3. You did not ask about lawyers, but you might be interested in the fact that, of the 166 heads of families in the gentry, 28 were barristers. (I am not including in the figures the tiny group of solicitors in this parliament.) Only two of these barristers were also businessmen. Thus the 26 businessmen and the 28 barristers, cancelling out the 2 overlapping cases, make a total of 52, or 31 per cent., of the gentry who were either businessmen or lawyers. That nearly one-third of the group was active in either business or the law seems to me a substantial finding. You will see from Table III how the other groups compare. Very few of the relatives of peers were lawyers—none of them were

businessmen, of course—while a large proportion of those unrelated to the landed class were either businessmen or professional men.

The figures for barristers may be a little high. I have tried to exclude men who were called to the bar but never practised. However, this fact was not always easy to establish, and I may have counted as barristers a few who did not have active careers in the law.

4. Table IV includes not only businessmen and barristers but those with minor business interests as well. The proportions now become very high: over half for the heads of families in both the gentry and the baronetage, while figures for the other groups also increase. Certainly Table IV makes it clear enough that the proportion of the landed class which had some connexion with business or law was very substantial.

One figure in Table IV may raise a question. Of those wholly unrelated to the landed class, I found that 76 per cent. had some connexion with business or the law. This leaves 24 per cent., or 38 men, who are, so to speak, unaccounted for. If these men belonged neither to the landed group nor to the business and professional group, you may wonder what was their means of livelihood. Most of these left-overs can, however, be explained by a more detailed analysis than it seems necessary to present here. In brief, a few of them were solicitors, quite a number were the sons of successful businessmen or professional men, and most of the rest were landowners who resembled the gentry in external characteristics though they did not happen to belong to the families included by Burke in his survey.

5. The connexion of members of the landed class with business can be shown in still another way. A substantial proportion of each group, in most cases just under or just over one-third, were descended from or had married into families which had or had had significant business interests. The information I have been able to find on this point is summarized in Table V. The connexion was not always close: in some cases the father or grandfather was a businessman; in other cases a distinguished family, even one with a high rank in the peerage, proved to have been established by a merchant or secured by marriage to a mercantile fortune several centuries before. The figures for the relatives of peers in Table V may be a little high, since I have taken account of certain great landed magnates who were actively concerned with exploiting their mineral resources or their urban real estate hold-

ings, men like Earl Fitzwilliam, the Marquess of Downshire, the Duke of Portland or the Duke of Bedford, all of whom had sons in this Parliament. Such individuals were not businessmen in the usual sense; yet their involvement in business enterprise seemed important enough so that, after some hesitation, I decided that it should be reflected in the statistics.

6. I mentioned earlier that the story came out much the same whether the gentry was defined narrowly or broadly. Table VI summarizes the information in Tables I–V for the gentry according to the narrowest and also according to the broadest definition. (To get the information on one page in a form where its purport could be easily grasped I have made the table add vertically, instead of horizontally like Tables I–V.) The first column, the 'Gentry by narrow definition', includes only the 234 men listed in Burke's *Landed Gentry* either as heads of families or sons of heads of families. The second column, the 'Gentry by broad definition', includes not only the 234 men listed in Burke but also the 129 men related to the baronetage, i.e. baronets and sons of baronets, and the 115 men more distantly related to the peerage, baronetage or gentry. The larger group is 478, just over double the smaller one.

The percentage figures in the two columns are extremely similar. The men in Burke resemble the men left out of Burke very closely, at least in the characteristics considered here, as soon as the figures are large enough to show some stability. This suggests that the broader definition of the gentry may be the more useful one, and that we should think of it as including not only the men listed by Burke but also the baronetage and those whose relationship to the landed class was more remote. At any rate, the general purport of the data is unmistakable. Further, the fact of the correspondence of the figures, regardless of whether a narrow or a broad definition is adopted, leads me to have increased confidence in their reliability.

TABLE I

	Businessmen		Not businessmen		Totals
	No.	%	No.	%	
Gentry:					
Heads of families	26	16	140	84	166
Eldest sons	—	—	35	100	35
Younger sons	6	18	27	82	33
Baronets:					
Heads of families	10	12	71	88	81
Eldest sons	1	5	21	95	22
Younger sons	7	27	19	73	26
Gentry and Baronets together:					
Heads of families	36	15	211	85	247
Eldest sons	1	2	56	98	57
Younger sons	13	22	46	78	59
Irish peers and sons of peers	—	—	180	100	180
More distantly related to peerage, baronetage or gentry	16	14	99	86	115
Wholly unrelated to peerage, baronetage or gentry	73	47	84	53	157
Entire Parliament	139	17	676	83	815

TABLE II

	Businessmen, or had minor connexions with business		Not connected with business in any way		Totals
	No.	%	No.	%	
Gentry:					
Heads of families	70	42	96	58	166
Eldest sons	5	14	30	86	35
Younger sons	9	27	24	73	33
Baronets:					
Heads of families	36	44	45	56	81
Eldest sons	6	27	16	73	22
Younger sons	10	38	16	62	26
Gentry and Baronets together:					
Heads of families	106	43	141	57	247
Eldest sons	11	19	46	81	57
Younger sons	19	32	40	68	59
Irish peers and sons of peers	49	27	131	73	180
More distantly related to peerage, baronetage or gentry	38	33	77	67	115
Wholly unrelated to peerage, baronetage or gentry	102	65	55	35	157
Entire Parliament	325	40	490	60	815

TABLE III

	Businessmen or barristers		Neither businessmen nor barristers		
	No.	%	No.	%	Totals
Gentry:					
Heads of families	52	31	114	69	166
Eldest sons	4	11	31	89	35
Younger sons	12	36	21	64	33
Baronets:					
Heads of families	18	22	63	78	81
Eldest sons	7	32	15	68	22
Younger sons	14	54	12	46	26
Gentry and Baronets together:					
Heads of families	70	28	177	72	247
Eldest sons	11	19	46	81	57
Heads of families	26	44	33	56	59
Irish peers and sons of peers	14	8	166	92	180
More distantly related to peerage, baronetage or gentry	38	33	77	67	115
Wholly unrelated to peerage, baronetage or gentry	100	64	57	36	157
Entire Parliament	259	32	556	68	815

TABLE IV

	Businessmen, men with minor business connexions, and barristers		No connexion with business and not barristers		Totals
	No.	%	No.	%	
Gentry:					
Heads of families	86	52	80	48	166
Eldest sons	7	20	28	80	35
Younger sons	13	39	20	61	33
Baronets:					
Heads of families	41	51	40	49	81
Eldest sons	9	41	13	59	22
Younger sons	16	62	10	38	26
Gentry and Baronets together:					
Heads of families	127	51	120	49	247
Eldest sons	16	28	41	72	57
Younger sons	29	49	30	51	59
Irish peers and sons of peers	55	31	125	69	180
More distantly related to peerage, baronetage or gentry	54	47	61	53	115
Wholly unrelated to peerage, baronetage or gentry	119	76	38	24	157
Entire Parliament	400	49	415	51	815

TABLE V

	Father or other relative in business		No known relative in business		
	No.	%	No.	%	Totals
Gentry:					
Heads of families	47	28	119	72	166
Eldest sons	10	29	25	71	35
Younger sons	14	42	19	58	33
Baronets:					
Heads of families	30	37	51	63	81
Eldest sons	9	41	13	59	22
Younger sons	12	46	14	54	26
Gentry and Baronets together:					
Heads of families	77	31	170	69	247
Eldest sons	19	33	38	67	57
Younger sons	26	44	33	56	59
Irish peers and sons of peers	67	37	113	63	180
More distantly related to peerage, baronetage or gentry	41	36	74	64	115
Wholly unrelated to peerage, baronetage or gentry	74	47	83	53	157
Entire Parliament	304	37	511	63	815

TABLE VI

SUMMARY OF CERTAIN INFORMATION IN TABLES I–V

	Gentry by narrow definition (234 men)		Gentry by broad definition (478 men)	
	No.	%	No.	%
Table I:				
Businessmen	32	14	66	14
Not businessmen	202	86	412	86
Table II:				
Businessmen, or had minor connexions with business	84	36	174	36
Not connected with business in any way	150	64	304	64
Table III:				
Businessmen or barristers	68	29	145	30
Neither businessmen nor barristers	166	71	333	70
Table IV:				
Businessmen, men with minor business connexions, and barristers	106	45	226	47
No connexion with business, and not barristers	128	55	252	53
Table V:				
Father or other relative in business	71	30	163	34
No known relative in business	163	70	315	66

BIBLIOGRAPHY

W. O. Aydelotte, "Voting patterns in the British House of Commons in the 1840s," *Comparative Studies in Society and History*, V (1963), 134–163.

Asa Briggs, *Victorian People*, Chicago, 1955.

———, "The language of 'class' in early Nineteenth Century England," in Asa Briggs and John Saville, eds., *Essays on Labour History, in Memory of G. D. H. Cole*, London, 1960.

Charlotte Erickson, *British Industrialists: Steel & Hosiery, 1850–1950*, Cambridge (England), 1959.

W. L. Guttsman, *The British Political Elite*, London, 1963.

Ralph E. Pumphrey, "The introduction of industrialists into the British peerage: A study in adaptation of a social institution," *American Historical Review*, LXV (1959), 1–16.

F. M. L. Thompson, *English Landed Society in the Nineteenth Century*, London, 1963.

THE PLACE OF BUSINESSMEN IN THE 19TH CENTURY FRENCH CLASS STRUCTURE *

David Landes

If there was a major turning point in European stratification systems during the early or middle nineteenth century—and entirely satisfactory evidence is not yet at hand to demonstrate the point—it is also clear that elements of the older type of system persisted well into the nineteenth century in many countries and perhaps even into our own time in a few. Some of these older elements—attitudes toward occupations, norms about social mobility—are described in this account by Landes of the place of businessmen in the class structure of nineteenth century France.

David Landes, who has taught at Columbia University and the University of California at Berkeley, has recently accepted an appointment in the History Department at Harvard. He is an economic historian whose main work has been on the banking and business institutions of nineteenth century France.

. . . In the French social structure the businessman had always held an inferior place. Three major forces conduced to this result. In the first place, he was detested from the start by the nobility, which rightly saw in him a subversive element. The aristocracy, its military and administrative functions slowly but surely ossifying in a new world of gunpowder and mercenaries, centralization and bureaucracy, turned at bay on its bourgeois adversaries and wreaked revenge with the strongest weapon it had left, prestige. Unable to compete with the driving spirit of these ambitious newcomers, unable to defeat them on their chosen ground of business with their chosen weapon, money, the nobility deliberately turned its back and tilted its nose. Against the practical, materialistic values of the businessman it set the consciously impractical, unmaterialistic values of the gentleman. Against the restless ambition of the parvenu, it placed the prestige of birth; against the mercurial efficacy of money, the solid stability of land; against the

* Reprinted from David Landes, "French Entrepreneurship and Industrial Growth in the 19th Century," *Journal of Economic History*, IX (1949), 45–61.

virtues of diligence and austerity, the dignity of leisure and the splendor
of pomp and circumstance.[1]

If anything, the revolutions of 1789 and 1830 strengthened this
attitude. Those few nobles who under the old regime had been active
as ironmasters, glass manufacturers, and so on, or had followed the
Colbertist tradition of encouragement of and investment in industry,
were now for the most part impoverished. To be sure, many of the new
generation, especially those whose titles were of recent vintage, were
to lend their names and prestige to entrepreneurial efforts and place
their capital in railroads, insurance, and other corporative enterprises.
But the aristocracy as a group had hardened its heart. The early years
of the July Monarchy saw a marked reaction against the new way and
the consecration of the myth of noble superiority, social, spiritual, and
even physical. One has only to read the flood of scornful literature
that followed the Revolution of 1830 to feel the bitterness approaching
revulsion on the part of the dispossessed toward anything smacking of
bourgeois business and money.[2]

That the entrepreneur was considerably influenced by the prestige
of this "superior" group is obvious from his continued efforts to rise
into its ranks, either directly or through marriage. For the same reasons,
the businessman was rare who did not acquire sooner or later a landed
estate, considered the safest of investments and an important criterion
of social status. Obviously, most of these new gentry were simply
absentee landlords. In some districts like Bordeaux the practice was just
about unanimous, and there shippers and merchants were at least as
well known for their vineyards and vintages as for their commercial
activities.[3] It is impossible to say with an precision how much of the
national wealth was diverted from business enterprise on this account,
but most writers are agreed that, whether made as a form of conspicuous consumption or for more serious reasons, such investments by
businessmen and nonbusinessmen were a significant obstacle to industrialization.

The hostility of the aristocracy would not have been enough in
itself, however, had it not been for the acceptance of this concept by
the nonbusiness elements of the *bourgeoisie*. This heterogeneous group,

[1] Cf. the succinct article, "Gentleman, Theory of the," in the *Encyclopedia of
the Social Sciences*.

[2] See, for example, the "dime novels" of Baron de Lamothe-Langon, especially
La Femme du banquier (2 vols.; Paris, 1832).

[3] Cf. the list of viticulturers given by E. Féret, *Supplément à la statistique
générale de la Gironde (partie vinicole)* (Bordeaux, 1880).

which is more easily defined negatively than positively since it includes almost everyone not falling into the small category of nobility or the large mass of the people, had developed in the course of centuries of slow ascension a scale of status heavily weighted with the prejudices of an aristocratic society. Of the multitude of professional groups that composed the *bourgeoisie,* the businessmen were generally relegated to the bottom of the ladder, other things being equal. In the last analysis, this social inferiority was what made possible the system of *charges* under the old regime, which by conferring on the *nouveaux riches* the prestige, security, and sometimes ennoblement of public office further depreciated the entrepreneurial classes and intensified their efforts to rise up and out of their "sordid" occupations.

These prejudices by no means died with the Revolution. Instead, the older *bourgeoise,* dominated by civil servants and the liberal professions, tended to stress their prestige in the face of rising capitalist elements. In this they were, generally speaking, quite successful, and the invidious distinction between the two groups has continued right up to the present, though with considerably less force since the economic and monetary disasters due to World War I. Considerations of status, moreover, were strengthened by such factors as the security of official or professional positions and the character of the French educational system, a primary force for social conservatism. For these reasons, the best talents in France almost invariably turned to the traditional honorific careers such as law, medicine, or government. This was true even of the children of businessmen. To be sure, the important entrepreneurs were succeeded by their own offspring, but here the importance of conserving the family heritage was a vital consideration, and, besides, great wealth has always excused many a fault. The average businessman was not so fortunate. Apparently, this "curse of *fonctionnarisme*" and the rush toward the liberal professions created in turn a certain pernicious instability on the lower entrepreneurial levels. One observer, struck by the age of the Flavigny wool firm of Elbeuf, was moved to write: "This inheritance of ownership in industry is something very rarely found in France; the designation 'and son', so common in England, is almost unknown in France. Is it the fault of our legislation or of our fickle character?" [4]

---

[4] Turgan, *Les grandes usines: études industrielles en France et à l'étranger* (Paris: Vol. I, Librairie Nouvelle, 1860; Vols. II–X, Michel Lévy, 1862–74), V, 71. The reference to legislation is to the French Code Civil, which, in imposing a relatively equal division of estates, necessitated the liquidation of business property whenever the heirs could not come to an agreement on continued operation.

BIBLIOGRAPHY

H. J. Habakkuk, "Family structure and economic change in nineteenth-century Europe," *Journal of Economic History*, 15 (1955), 1–12.

David Landes, "French Business and the Businessman: A Social and Cultural Analysis," in Edward Mead Earle, ed., *Modern France*, Princeton, 1951.

William Miller, ed., *Men in Business*, Cambridge (Mass.), 1952.

John E. Sawyer, "Strains in the Social Structure of Modern France," in Edward Mead Earle, *Modern France*, Princeton, 1951.

SOCIAL CLASS OF CAMBRIDGE UNIVERSITY ALUMNI OF THE 18TH AND 19TH CENTURIES *

Hester Jenkins and D. Caradog Jones

For a very long time, in nearly all European societies, schools and universities have been instruments by which some upper-class families have maintained the social-class position of their children. At the same time, these schools and universities have been open, to some extent, to people of talent from the middle and lower classes. Probably the extent to which social mobility has been occurring through the universities has been increasing since the eighteenth century. The conclusions of the study reported here supports this view for the graduates of Cambridge University. It also shows how the upper classes in England were shifting from landowning and church and governmental functions to more diversified industrial, commercial, and professional functions. . . .

Hester Jenkins and D. Caradog Jones are British sociologists. The late Mr. Jones was Editor of the Social Survey of Merseyside, *co-author with Professor A. M. Carr-Saunders of* The Social Structure of England and Wales, *and a long-time student of the structure of occupations and the processes of social mobility in Great Britain.*

The following are some of the chief conclusions reached as a result of this study, the source of the material for the first three periods, 1752–

* Reprinted from the article of the same title in *British Journal of Sociology*, I (1950), 93–116, published by Routledge and Kegan Paul Ltd.

99, 1800–49, 1850–99, being Dr. J. A. Venn's *Alumni Cantabrigienses,* and for the years 1937–8, data supplied by college tutors for an inquiry into *University Education and Business.*

(1) A high proportion of the fathers of Cambridge men during the latter half of the eighteenth and the whole of the nineteenth centuries were of the land-owning class and nearly one-third were parsons. The Church was also the profession favoured by as many as three out of every five of Cambridge men in the first two periods reviewed and by nearly two out of five in the third period. By 1937–8 a phenomenal expansion had taken place, among both fathers and sons, in the proportion of commercial and industrial occupations entered with a corresponding decline under the headings of church and land-owning.

(2) There is evidence of an appreciable fall in the second half of the nineteenth century in the proportion represented by the non-earning land-owning class among those who sent their sons to Cambridge and in the proportion of sons who were themselves eventually so classed. This was balanced by a rise in the proportions of sons sent by other classes of the population to Cambridge during the same period.

(3) An increasing proportion of entrants, rising to more than one-half in 1850–99, had been educated in one of the twenty-three foremost public schools and another 30 per cent in that period came from other public schools. A substantial proportion of parents must therefore have been drawn from the relatively small class in the country who were in a position to pay the high fees necessary to cover a public school and university education. For the rest, no doubt, it often meant a considerable sacrifice. Many of the clergy, for instance, sent their sons to the smaller and less costly schools in consequence. No nonconformist was admitted until 1850. In short, the university population was highly selected and narrowly restricted, and opportunities for climbing the social ladder by this means were correspondingly limited. After 1900 men from the new type of secondary school maintained by Local Education Authorities began to find their way to Cambridge, so that a decline is observed in the proportion of public school men among the alumni from 82 per cent in 1850–99 to 68 per cent in 1937–8.

(4) The men who gained the highest distinction at Cambridge in proportion to their numbers in two out of the three periods studied were the products of the less conspicuous grammar schools, not the public schools. The order of academic success, in fact, was

$$g, \quad P_2, \quad P_1, \quad p,$$

the other public schools doing better than the more famous. This is explained by the fact that only the best boys from the g schools, and in some degree from the P_2 schools also, found their way to Cambridge, often with the help of scholarships.

(5) The sons of professional men—lawyers, doctors, and school-masters—had the best record at Cambridge, and the sons of parsons came next. Men from homes of the land-owning class, 70 per cent of whom were educated in first-grade public schools, were at the bottom in each of the three periods studied.

(6) When we proceed to consider distinction in afterlife, those educated at the more famous public schools (P_1) outstripped the others. This success may have been due in part to the self-confidence acquired and the training for leadership given in these schools; in part it may have been the result of school and family influence, which may be direct or indirect: a man stands a better chance of a good post simply because he is known to have come from a school or family of high social standing.

(7) There seems to be little doubt that such influence was respon-sible for securing posts of distinction for sons of the land-owning class, since over 80 per cent were either placed in only the third class at Cambridge or they failed to take any degree at all; yet 54 per cent of this same group of relative failures, academically, were found later in life enjoying positions of first- or second-class distinction. This pro-portion was much in excess of that observed in any comparable aca-demic group of relative failures whose fathers were not classed among land-owners. The evidence further suggests that school and family influence alone may secure for a man a position of grade 2, but not of grade 1, distinction.

(8) Leaving out of account the experience of the exceptional and highly favoured land-owning class, it can be safely asserted of the rest, that conspicuous success at Cambridge was a general rule followed by success in afterlife. On the other hand, a fairly high proportion of men with second-class degrees failed to secure posts of any distinction later. The sons of professional men did well on the whole in afterlife, main-taining their high record at the university; but the sons of parsons fared badly, the proportion of their distinctions being low.

(9) A high proportion of sons tended to enter the same profession as their fathers. Since there has always been a fairly close connection between the older universities and the Established Church, it is not surprising that ordinands should be strongly represented among Cam-bridge alumni. They did rather better at the University than in after

life; the proportion who achieved subsequent distinction was at no period higher than 12 or 15 per cent. This may have been due in part to relatively few opportunities for distinction in the Church.

BIBLIOGRAPHY

C. Arnold Anderson and Miriam Schnaper, *School and Society in England: Social Backgrounds of Oxford and Cambridge Students,* Washington, D.C., 1952.

N. G. Annan, "The Intellectual Aristocracy," in J. H. Plumb, ed., *Studies in Social History,* London, 1955.

Theodor Geiger, "An Historical Study of the Origins and Structure of the Danish Intelligentsia," *British Journal of Sociology,* I (1950), 209–220.

Nicholas Hans, *New Trends in Education in the Eighteenth Century,* London, 1951.

Edward C. Mack, *Public Schools and British Opinion, 1780–1860,* London, 1936.

CHANGE AND THE STRATIFICATION SYSTEM IN RUSSIA, GREAT BRITAIN, AND THE UNITED STATES *

Bernard Barber

Three cases of changing stratification systems are described in this excerpt from a systematic comparative analysis of social stratification. The Russian case is one in which the change was from the caste to the open-class type and by means of violent revolution and thoroughgoing social planning. The British and American cases are ones in which the changes are substantial but still within type, in this case the open-class type, and occur by gradual, peaceful, and often unintended means.

Bernard Barber, who has taught sociology at Harvard and Smith College, is Professor at Barnard College, Columbia University. In addi-

* Reprinted from Bernard Barber. *Social Stratification: A Comparative Analysis of Structure and Process,* New York: Harcourt, Brace & World, 1957, (Ch. 17, Social Change and Social Stratification Systems).

tion to his book and articles on social stratification, he has written
Science and the Social Order.

Russia

Social change occurs not only at varying rates of speed but as the
result of varying amounts of social planning. In this case, we have an
example of a society where the change from a basically caste type of
stratification system to an open-class one has been brought about by
revolution and by over-all state social planning.[1]

In legal terms, pre-revolutionary Russia was, like eighteenth-century
France, an "estate" society. The law defined special rights and duties
for each of three estates: the clergy, hereditary nobility, and a third
estate consisting of peasants and town-dwelling merchants and workers.
In terms of social stratification, pre-revolutionary Russia was, again like
eighteenth-century France, basically of the caste type, but with a much
larger admixture of open-class elements. Indeed, since Russia had begun
to industrialize, and this with increasing speed in the twentieth century,
the admixture of open-class elements was large enough that some
scholars have argued that Russia was already more nearly an open-class
than a caste society. Certainly there was a small but increasing number
of industrialists, merchants, and skilled workers; moreover, many upper-
class intellectuals were ardently devoted to universalistic values and
ideologies. Hence the appeal of various democratic, constitutional,
socialist, and Marxist social philosophies. Many of the mobile bourgeois,
however, did not approve in principle of social mobility for all but,
like their eighteenth-century prototypes in France, wanted only to
move into the hereditary noble class themselves. Just how much actual
social mobility and institutionalized approval existed in pre-revolutionary Russia, we do not know. We can only venture the estimate that
these open-class elements were probably somewhat subordinate to the

[1] Our discussion of this case is based primarily on the following: N. S.
Timasheff, "Vertical Mobility in Communist Society," *Amer. Sociol. Rev.*, 50
(1944), 9–21; Barrington Moore, Jr., *Soviet Politics—The Dilemma of Power*,
Harvard U. Press, 1950, and *Terror and Progress, USSR*, Harvard U. Press, 1954;
W. W. Rostow and others, *The Dynamics of Soviet Society*, Norton, 1953; Alex
Inkeles, "Stratification and Mobility in the Soviet Union," *Amer. Sociol. Rev.*,
15 (1950), 465–79; Robert A. Feldmesser, "The Persistence of Status Advantages
in Soviet Russia," *Amer. J. Sociol.*, 59 (1953), 19–27; and S. V. Utechin, "Social
Stratification and Social Mobility in the U.S.S.R.," in *Transactions of the Second
World Congress of Sociology*, International Sociological Association, London,
1954.

basically caste type of stratification system. This is not to imply, of course, that over the longer run there would not have occurred inevitably a slow and gradual increase in the open-class elements, eventuating in a basically open-class society.

But social change in Russia was not to take place gradually or peaceably. A violent revolution initiated, and social planning has carried to completion, basic changes in every part of Russian society: in the organization of production, in the property system, in the political and legal systems, in education, in science, in the family, in religion, and, not least of all, in values and ideologies. Just how the revolution was begun or the social transformation completed is not, like many great historical events, entirely clear even to those who have studied the history and sociology of Russian society most intensively. However, the fundamental importance of Marxist-Leninist theory and of Communist Party organization in initiating and consolidating the revolution is unmistakable. In the beginning, in fact, Marxist-Leninist theory gave the revolution a utopian cast. It proclaimed that such fundamental social structures as the stratification system, the state bureaucracy, and the family would ultimately be unnecessary. Eventually, however, though basic changes in these and other structures were made, the Russians have had to recede from their utopian views or at least announce the postponement of the realization into the indefinite future.

Even in a revolution, basic social changes do not occur overnight, nor sometimes even in a single generation. The deaths and destruction, the expropriation of property, and the social disfranchisement of the formerly privileged classes did, in the period of revolutionary violence and immediately thereafter, cause a great increase in both upward and downward social mobility in Russia. But as Lenin recognized in his "Testament," there is a limit to the extent to which "new" men can immediately take the place of the "old" social groups. It takes time especially to train technical specialists; it also takes time to allow "new" men to gain the necessary experience even in positions that require no special technical training. Lenin and the other revolutionary leaders were compelled, therefore, to allow many of the former middle- and upper-class industrial, civil-service, and free-professional experts to remain in their old positions. Looking to the future, however, the Communists began to train their own experts. During the 1920's, special privileges in education were given to industrial workers and their children. This facilitated the social mobility of these "proletarian" groups. Undoubtedly, though, some of the children of those members of the old upper classes who had been retained in high positions were able to profit from their family advantages and maintain unchanged the social class position in which they were born. That is the consequence, or "price," of preserving some stable continuity in a society even though it has undergone a fundamental social revolution.

Probably the period of maximum social mobility and of the most rapid increase in open-class norms and ideologies occurred in Russia in the late twenties, the thirties, and the forties, the period in which there was the greatest proportionate expansion of Russia's industrial, governmental, military, scientific, and educational systems. The absolute number of middle- and higher-ranking positions in Soviet society was vastly increased in this period, and probably the proportion of these positions relative to the lower ones was also somewhat increased. These increases created a vast expansion of the opportunities for social mobility of both large and small degree. Along with the expansion resulting from industrialization, the recurrent "purges" of pre-revolutionary groups from the higher-ranking positions also enlarged the opportunities for social mobility during the thirties and forties.

By now, Soviet society has settled down with an open-class stratification system very much like that of the other industrialized countries of Europe and in the United States. The educational system is now as much one of the key elements in the processes of mobility in Russia as it is in other open-class industrial societies that require and provide opportunities for individual achievement. Actual access to what is formally a universally available education system is influenced by social class position in Russia as it is in other open-class societies. The settling down of Russian society probably has lessened, relative to the thirties and forties and earlier, the amount of social mobility that now occurs. Nevertheless, there is still a considerable amount of social mobility. A safe estimate of the patterns of mobility in Russia now and at least for the foreseeable future would be that they are much like what exists in other open-class societies. Probably a fairly large minority of the population remains in the class into which it was born; another large minority moves up or down in relatively small degree; and a small minority moves up or down in the class structure in large degree. Until we have better comparative evidence for Russia and other industrial countries which will reveal subtle differences in the amount and processes of mobility, the safest estimate of the Russian stratification system is that it consists of norms, structure, and processes basically similar to those of other open-class industrial societies in Europe and the United States. That is the estimate supported by all the good evidence now in hand.

Great Britain

It has often been said that during and since the end of World War II Great Britain has gone through a "social revolution." Great social changes have indeed occurred during the last fifteen years in many different parts of the society, and these have been important to nearly every member of the society. But are these changes "revolutionary"? In some sense, perhaps they are. But not in the sense of involving fundamental changes *of type* in any of the major social institutions. The changes have been planned and carried through by means of long-established democratic political techniques. They have been agreed to, on the whole, by the adherents of both of the major political parties. In short, they have been built on long-standing social consensus. In this case, then, we shall consider recent changes in the stratification system of Great Britain as examples of changes within a stable and institutionalized open-class system.[2]

As we have suggested earlier, Great Britain may have had a predominantly open-class type of stratification since at least the early-middle part of the nineteenth century. All during that century and continuing up to the present, a series of incremental changes have tended to make the stratification system approximate ever more nearly the open-class type. Social change has often not come as fast or as easily as many Britons wished; there have always been many people to criticize

[2] There is no single book that discusses recent changes in Britain's stratification system as a whole. An excellent study of processes and amounts of mobility and of the importance of the educational system may be found in David V. Glass, ed., *Social Mobility in Britain*, Routledge and Kegan Paul, London, 1954. A journalistic and somewhat hostile account of recent events in Britain is contained in Roy Lewis and Angus Maude, *The English Middle Classes*, Knopf, 1950. See also the valuable material in G. D. H. Cole, *Studies in Class Structure*, Routledge and Kegan Paul, London, 1955, especially Chap. 3, "The Social Structure of England"; Chap. 5, "Elites in British Society"; and Chap. 6, "British Class Structure in 1951." In Chap. 3 Cole attempts a sketchy comparison of English class structure in 1851 and 1951. An inclusive but unsystematic discussion of the English stratification system and of some recent change may also be found in T. H. Pear, *English Social Differences*, Allen and Unwin, London, 1955. Finally, see John Bonham, *The Middle Class Vote*, Faber and Faber, London, 1954, especially the last chapter, "Who Cares for the Middle Class?"

the persistence of caste elements in British society. But the general direction of change in the stratification system has been constant. And in this perspective especially, the post-World War II changes in Britain represent another large increment of a long trend of change within the open-class type of stratification system. During the last one hundred and fifty years, for example, the availability of education, both as to amount and quality, has been spreading in Britain. The recent increases in scholarships, the improvement of schools for the poorer groups, and the "opening up" of the "public schools" and of Oxford and Cambridge, then, are social changes that build upon earlier and similar changes in the educational system. Further, the diminution of family advantages for the maintenance of high social class position through the levying of progressive income and inheritance taxes is also not new to Britain, though these instruments of an open-class society have been applied with increased force in the postwar period. Finally, if the political influence of the lower classes reached a peak in Britain after the war through the Labor Party and the Labor Government, this too was a development founded on a long history of slowly increasing political influence among the lower classes.

A long series of peaceable, slow, and interrelated social changes have made the stratification system of Great Britain approach ever more nearly, though not absolutely achieve, the open-class type. There seems to have occurred a general "flattening" of the class structure, that is, there has been a trend toward relatively fewer people in the upper and lower classes. The proportion of people in that broad range of the class structure ideologically defined as "the middle classes," has been increasing. Differences of evaluation and of the associated social privileges still exist, but they are less obvious than formerly because more subtly graded and more subtly expressed. The rise in the standard of living of the lower and lower-middle classes—their better food, better education, better health, better housing, and better clothes—has not only increased their chances for social mobility but has eliminated some of the most striking of the former symbols of their social class inferiority. Speaking of education, for example, G. D. H. Cole has recently said:

The educational policies to which Great Britain stands committed under the Butler Education Act of 1944 involve an increasing equalization of opportunity, though not by any means a complete levelling—for they leave the "Public" Schools intact, and we are still a very long way off "parity of esteem" between the different types of state secondary school, even apart from wide disparities in actual ages at leaving. The trend is, however, clearly towards a lessening of educational inequality and towards a wider diffusion of opportunity for the gifted children of poor parents.[3]

Or, speaking in general, an editorial writer in *The Economist* has written: "The reduction of the inequality of wealth and welfare is, to judge by the evidence, one of the strongest passions of the British people in this generation. To a quite remarkable extent it is shared by the comfortable, whose eyes are open to the fact that any progress toward equality must be at their expense." [4] Thus, there seem to be on all sides stronger sentiments of approval of social mobility; equality of opportunity for individual achievement in all socially valued roles is now a more common ideal in all social classes. Great Britain, then, is not now a classless society; nor has she undergone a major social revolution such as that of 1789 in France or of 1917 in Russia. She has, rather, taken somewhat longer steps than at other times in the past down a path of change toward a more nearly open-class type of stratification system—a path she has been following for a long time.

The United States

Our final case is the United States. The United States is an example of a society in which the changes of the stratification system are changes *within type*. In our discussion of various concrete aspects of the stratification system, it has been impossible to separate the analysis of structure and stability from the analysis of process and change. We have, therefore, discussed change as well as stability in the American stratification system in such chapters as those on symbolic indicators, on class consciousness and class organization, on class socialization, on the processes of mobility, and on the amounts of mobility.

Just how much change there has been in the American open-class stratification system we cannot precisely say. Nor can we be absolutely sure about the general direction of the change that has occurred within that type. The social changes taking place recently may, as some Americans have thought, be in the direction of a somewhat less open-class society. But it seems more likely that these changes have generally strengthened the conditions necessary for an open-class stratification system and made that system a little bit more realizable in practice. For

[3] Cole, *Studies in Class Structure*, p. 76.
[4] *The Economist*, Feb. 4, 1950, p. 245.

example, there is no evidence that Americans now approve any less of social mobility than they ever have in the past. Indeed, the studies . . . all point to a persistence of open-class sentiments and aspirations, even in the face of widespread social depression or individual "failure." And some seem to point to an equally persistent amount of social mobility. Even the Negroes, with regard to whom the caste elements in American society have always been strongest, have recently won a set of social improvements among which not the least is the weakening of the prejudices against them among their white fellow Americans.

Certainly we can point to a number of social processes and social changes that have probably served to strengthen the American open-class stratification system. Education and educational opportunity, though still not equal for all, are changing in the direction of greater availability and equality. Political and other forms of social influence are becoming somewhat less unequally distributed among the social classes. The development of labor union organizations and of their participation in national and local politics has been one of the basic sources of the reduction of political and social inequality among the classes. As in England, the American tax system serves to diminish the differential advantages provided by accumulated family wealth; this system has recently become an even more effective instrument of this open-class function. Science and technology have continually been creating in American society new opportunities for entrepreneurial ability and new jobs requiring valued social and technical knowledge and skill. And these in turn provide continuing opportunities for social mobility. In general, conservative or reactionary inequalitarian ideologies and movements have either been lacking or strikingly unsuccessful in their appeals for support. Other social changes have at least not weakened, and sometimes they have actively strengthened, the set of conditions required for enlarging the realization of an open-class type of stratification system in the United States.

To many people, the account given above of social change and the American stratification system will seem excessively optimistic. But perhaps it will seem so only because Americans have tended to have utopian expectations with regard to their stratification system and have been impatient of any hindrance to completely free social mobility. We have analyzed some of the reasons why such mobility does not occur. Therefore Americans can be optimistic without being utopian. Optimism, of course, does not mean that they should be complacent. Because the stratification system is a system in process, continuous social action of many different kinds is required either to maintain it in the state Americans desire or to improve it. They must therefore pay constant attention to the social arrangements and policies that foster the kind of stratification system and change they want. Increasingly, as social science develops, social change can be planned and foreseen. The choice for Americans now is not between an open-class and a cast type of stratification system; it is among degrees of approximation to the open-class system and to the American ideals. Perhaps this is also true now for societies all around the world.

BIBLIOGRAPHY

D. V. Glass, ed., *Social Mobility in Britain*, London, 1954.

S. M. Lipset and Reinhard Bendix, *Social Mobility in Industrial Society*, Berkeley and Los Angeles, 1959.

B. B. Misra, *The Indian Middle Classes: Their Growth in Modern Times*, London, 1961.

Kaare Svalastoga, *Prestige, Class, and Mobility*, Copenhagen, 1959.

Michael Young, *The Rise of the Meritocracy, 1870–2033, An Essay on Education and Equality*, London, 1958.